What Others Are Saying About This Critical Issue

"Linda Raney Wright identifies the real crises. If the church responds to the challenge, the nation's social, moral and family problems wouldn't loom so large because evangelism deals with the heart of those problems not merely the symptoms.'

Dr. Luis Palau
International Evangelist

"Evangelism is stuck in a time warp which propagates methology out of step with the realities of the secular culture. Linda Raney Wright sets out not to curse the darkenss but to shed light on the principles of effective successful relationships that people need to hear the music before they hear the words. Her book is a wake up call, a reality chick for believers seeking to reach those who need to know Jesus.

"Her analysis of the unbeliever and his/her perception of Christ is worth the price of the book. Exposure to this book will greatly enhance your understanding of the dynamics of sharing your faith. Implementation of these biblical insights should get believers building bridges with redemptive impact. I heartily encourage you to read this highly creative and unusual book. You will be greatly enoucraged by its content."

Joe Aldrich,
Pres. Multnomah Bible College,
and Biblical Seminary
Author, Lifestyle Evangelism

"Christians who are serious about influencing others for our Lord Jesus Christ will be both challenged and helped by this insightful volume. We desperately need to love those who are helpless, harassed and lost as Jesus loves them."

Paul Cedar,
President, Evangelical Free Church of America

"I have been waiting for a message like this to come out for the last five years. Linda has always been one step ahead of the other Christian Communicators. This book leads the pack. I hope Christians will take to heart the necessity for us to get our perspective back and look at the non-believers as friends, not enemies."

Florence Littauer
President, CLASS Speakers,
Author/Speaker

"This is an important book! The current "cultural war" in America has often hindered evangelism by making Christians demonize the oppisition, rather than seeing them as people for whom Christ died. The crucial point in this book is that christians need to view non-believers as persons who are lost, not enimies to be attacked. This book may be controversial.

Leighton Ford,
International Evangelist

"In Christianity's Crisis in Evangelism Linda Raney Wright provides a desperately needed warning to Christians who love their fellow humanbeings. What she has to say is right on the lost to a saving knowledge of Christ. It is equally relevant for those Chirstians who love thier country and seek a more just society that will bring greather good to all. Too often we seem perversely determined to antagonize those we seek to win and thus drive them farther from the gospel or a truly good society. Examples are legion. We bear witness to a God who love sinners so much that he chose to become human like us and then die for us so that we might be forgiven of our sin and transformed into truly good beings. We come across as those who hate humanity and, especially, all we consider sinners. Instead of loving them we shoot them. Instead of giving ourselves to help them, we despise them, keep distance from them and by our malicious condemnation of them incite others to hate them and destroy them. Instead of defending the unborn and their freedom to live, we come across as destructive of freedom of women. Instead of supporting the right to exercise one's religion freely with persecution, we are seen as working to force our religion by law on all tohers. We have replaced 'the offence of the cross' with the offence of our own stupidity, hatred, brutality and narrow minded sectarianism. Linda Raney Wright sums it all up in her final paragraph.

"As we deliver the message, we should remember that many will respond if our prayers and lives are Spirit-powered and our message is loving, relevant and convincing. If our listener is offended let's continue to make sure that the true gospel is the only offense, not our life, our judgments, the issues, the viewpoint about country, our sin, our own unChristlike attitude, our inadequate communication, our exclusivity, our erroneous view of the non-Christian, our lack of love, our intolerance, our isolation, our selectivity, our morals, our preoccupation with self and family, our hypocrisy, or our sloppy thinking. Together, let's clean house.'"

Kenneth S. Kantzer
Professor, New Testament,
Trinity International University

"Linda Raney Wright offers wise and compassionate counsel for reaching the lost. Giving her counsel the ring of authenticity, she speaks not as a theoretician, but as a practitioner. The reader will be well reawarded."

Dr. Robert E. Coleman
Director, Institute of Evangelism
at The Billy Graham Center,
Wheaton Professor of Evangelism School
of World Missions and Evangelism,
Trinity International University

"Linda Raney Wright hits the nail on the head. Too many Christians are emphasizing the public fight to save society from evil influences—at the expense of saving the lost. What's needed is more loving, one-on-one evangelism. Wright's message is compelling, convicting, and timely."

Fred Barnes
Senior Editor, The New Republic
A Regular on TV's McLaughlin Group

"I'm glad somebody said it...and nobody could have said it better! Linda Raney Wright has written a book that should be a call to the Church of Christ not to forget that we are 'here for them.' In our desire to do good things...we have forgotten the most important thing. Read this book! We need to hear its message so that the world can hear Christ's message.

Steve Brown
Professor of Preaching
Reformed Theological Seminary
President, Key Life Network

"Those of us keenly interested in evangelism—and particularly concerned with the American church today—are grateful to Linda Raney Wright for this licid, thoughtful analysis of the contemporary chruch scene as it related to obeying the biblical, evangelistic mandate.

"This book will help us to open our eyes and recognize, as the author so clearly indicated, that evangelism is indeed in crisis. But, she doesn't leave us there; she shows us God's pattern for our response to a society, whom He deeply loves and to whom we as well are called to love. Here is a courageous and needed call to responsible action to all of us who call ourselves believers."

Ted W. Engstrom
President Emeritus, World Vision

"This book hits the proverbial nail on the head. We are not reaching the lost because we are not loving them."

Lorry Lutz
International Coordinator
AD 2000 Woman's Track

"The issues raised in this book are absolutely critical to the success of evangelism in the decades ahead. Unless we quit viewing non-believers as the enemy we will never possess the senistivity we need to introduce them to the Savior."

Paul Eshleman, Dirctor
The JESUS Film Project

"I don't believe I have ever read a book on evangelism which so gently but forcefully hit me in the solar plexus! It is os much easier to bemoan the evils of our day and to assume that "sinners" don't want to be annoyed by any attempt I might make to evangelize them, than to recognize, as Jesus so often did, that the most unlikely person just might be the one most prepared for the Good News. This book is not simply about evangelism. It is a book which changes us—the readers—and thus prepares us to be the evangelists Christ hs called us to be. It is must reading!"

Roberta Winter
US Center for World Missions

Christianity's Crisis in Evangelism

Christianity's Crisis in Evangelism

Going Where the People Are

Linda Raney Wright

142500

VISION™
HOUSE
PUBLISHING, INC.
Gresham, Oregon 97030

CHRISTIANITY'S CRISIS IN EVANGELISM
© 1995 by Linda Raney Wright

Published by Vision House Publishing, Inc.
1217 NE Burnside, Suite 403
Gresham, Oregon 97030

Printed in the United States of America.

International Standard Book Number: 1-885305-24-9

95 96 97 98 99 00 01 02 03 04 - 10 9 8 7 6 5 4 3 2 1

Dedication

This book is dedicated to pastors, evangelists, and intercessors around the world.

And to personal friends who have played an important role in my life and in the furtherance of the gospel of our Lord: Nancy Pfaff, Dr. Corinne Allen, and Kathleen Santucci.

And especially to William D. Raney.
My brother Bill is handicapped (aren't we all?) with cerebral palsy and a hearing deficiency. He came to Christ at age twenty and since that time has, through deaf singing groups, church witnessing, inviting friends to church, personal confrontation, and the wearing of wildly imaginative Christian T-shirts, told the world that Christ makes a difference. Probably more than anyone I know, he has labored, with difficulty, to exemplify Christ and to be a messenger of the gospel to others.
Brother Bill . . . lead the way!

Contents

Acknowledgments

Any project such as this involves help from many sources. I want to express my profound gratitude to all who contributed in ways large and small, especially to the following:

Claudia and Clark Fisher, Kathleen and Hugo Santucci, Nancy Pfaff, Heather Amuny, Dave Holden, and Bob and Anita Friedman for reading and critiquing the manuscript.

Betty and Ed Tafflinger, Marilyn Adamson, and Bobby Mason for contributing valuable ideas along the way.

David Holden for the title suggestion.

Betsy Rogers for typing.

Rusty Wright for typing, editing, and encouraging.

Liz Heaney, an accomplished editor, who deserves much credit for the final, readable version of this book. A hearty thank you.

John Van Diest, my publisher, for responding to God's prompting (in the middle of the night!) and asking me to write this book. Thank you for listening.

The faithful staff at Vision House Publishing for their tremendous efforts in the publishing process.

Over one hundred dedicated prayer warriors who interceded with God on behalf of this book.

Other Books by Linda Raney Wright

Raising Children
Success Helper
Staying on Top When Things Go Wrong
Why Not?
How to Unlock the Secrets of Love, Sex, and Marriage
Secrets of Successful Humor
A Cord of Three Strands
Spiritual Warfare and Evangelism
Hope for the Sick and Hurting (Good Days, Bad Days)

Chapter One

Christianity's Crisis in Evangelism

I recently asked ten Christians from various denominations, "What do you think of non-Christians?" They answered:

1. "They are rebellious. I think they're destroying our country."

2. "They are getting worse and worse."

3. "They are probably the same as always in conduct or philosophy, but they are more vocal against Christians."

4. "I hope God will judge them."

5. "I hope Jesus comes soon and takes me out of here."

6. "The evil of non-Christians is increasing."

7. "I think God loves them, but I think they have rejected him."

8. "Gosh, I don't know how to answer that question, but isn't it awful what's happening in our country?"

9. "It's obvious they're not interested in God."

10. "I don't know."

These comments reflect the current crisis in evangelism. Many Christians seem to view the nonbeliever as less than human. We no longer view non-Christians as lost—we've come to see them as the enemy, and some have launched a frontal attack against those we see as evil. I'm gravely concerned about our lack of compassion for those Christ came to save.

In a word: Evangelism is in crisis.

Christians today hear that the communal family and moral values are being threatened. Some of our privileges and rights as Christians have been challenged.

Christian communicators, via speeches, letters, campaigns, and articles, are calling us to confront societal issues. As a result, many of us have begun to revise our opinion about those who oppose our points of view: abortionists are not only murderers, they are anti-God; in the U.S.A., the American Civil Liberties Union is not only liberal, it's intrinsically evil; feminists have wrong motives and have refused God's ways; homosexuals are not only immoral, they are anti-Christ, and on and on it goes.

Much of our communication is taken up with information about those who oppose us. We have identified large groups, categorizing and labeling them. We have at times defined these people indirectly and directly as anti-God, anti-family.

We see them as people who deliberately and knowingly make sinful choices. We believe they are rebellious and have an agenda to destroy us and our values. We suppose that none of them would be interested in hearing the gospel.

Recently I surveyed a number of committed Christians about how they spend their time on various issues: financial management (because of the fear the economy will fail), abortion, pornography, protests, correspondence to congresspersons, school-related issues, homosexuality, family concerns, etc. My survey included questions about how much time was spent thinking, praying, talking, worrying, contributing financially to, and doing something about these issues. Other questions included: How much time do you spend with social and family issues? How much time do you spend learning about non-Christians and their motives and beliefs? As a result of this informal poll, I discovered *much more time was spent saving the morals, saving the country, and saving the family than in saving the lost.*

Those who defend this position frequently quote 2 Chronicles 7:14, "If my people, who are called by my name, will humble themselves and pray and seek my face and turn from their wicked ways, then will I hear from heaven and will forgive their sin and will heal their land." This verse has been used to support calls for national repentance and, under the circumstances, has been enormously important. But have we forgotten that although Scripture gives important principles on family and nation, this teaching is not to eclipse a more essential focus—the gospel. The good news is to every person on earth who would choose God whether or not the family or nation from which they came is God honoring.

Today many Christians are confused about priorities. We wonder, Do I fight for my Christian values or do I share my faith? Should I focus on my family or blitz the neighborhood with the gospel? Do I become an evangelical Christian activist? How in the world do we bridge the widening gap between the gospel and non-Christians?

The church needs to do some evangelistic house-cleaning. Our system for delivering the Good News of Jesus Christ, full of cobwebs and dust, is breaking down and deteriorating.

An Us vs. Them Mentality

Many Christians believe we need to become moral and God honoring. With cheerleading enthusiasm we hail: "Let's get back to morals in our country"; "Let's return to the principles of our country's founders"; "Let's get back to family values."

Like those sitting on the sidelines with little interest in the game being played, many non-Christians see no need for such a change, especially when Christ's love and forgiveness are absent in such opinions. Non-Christians feel distanced and cut off from dialogue with Christians because of the gap in values and perspectives. They feel they have been labeled or judged unfairly and many are angry. They resent the accusations that they are destroying the nation. We are alienating those Christ came to save.

Sadly, many Christians have bought the idea that the non-Christian is the enemy whom we need to fear, confront, and defeat. Other Christians determine to avoid contact with non-Christians by establishing lifestyles which remove them by and large from secular influence. Both positions are deadly. Without realizing it, we begin to see everyone but ourselves as faceless, unfeeling, all of one mold, anti-God, and expressly evil.

I know something of this attitude. One night as I was driving down the incline near my house, a car pulled out of a driveway and blocked both lanes. A crowd of older teenage boys got out of the car, very slowly walked around it, and got in on the other side while several cars, mine included, waited for them to finish this parade and move out of the street.

Do you know what popped into my mind? Immediately I labeled them rebellious teenagers, doing whatever they wanted without respect for people. I honked my horn to hurry them along and to display my displeasure at all the selfish teenagers in the world.

Immediately I felt ashamed. In two minutes I had dumped all my accumulated anger toward "the unrighteous" on these kids, completely losing sight of God's love for them. My horn reflected the anger of personal inconvenience, not the loving concern of an ambassador of Christ.

I recognized, too, that I was a product of the American Christian environment which has in recent years, perhaps without meaning to, bred fear and anger toward those who don't embrace Christianity and the gospel.

Where Have We Gone Wrong?

It's not just our view of non-Christians that threatens the evangelism enterprise. We are sending out fewer missionaries because we want more money for ourselves. The pleasures of life distract us and our lust for more consumes our focus and our time. We are no longer concerned about evangelism and our confidence in witnessing is on the decrease. Even the gospel message is being redefined.

Consider the evangelistic issues and priorities that are being challenged and attacked:

Evangelism Priority	Attack
Concern for the lost	Hostility (save the nation, save the family, save the morals—rather than save the lost).
Time given to evangelism	Distraction, materialism.
Gospel message	Confusion over what constitutes the gospel.
Full work force in evangelism	Lack of respect for the full work force (i.e. minorities, disabled, women, etc.).
Resources for evangelism	Recession, materialism.
Gospel for all	White churches and some ministries moving to suburbs, large parts of population (ethnic/poor) untouched. Groups such as secular media, humanist, liberal, feminist, American Civil Liberties Union, New-Age, etc. largely seen as enemies and set apart from evangelism.
Group responsibility	Teaching that those who are supposed to be saved will be, with or without a witness.
Prayer and spiritual warfare	Not emphasized in evangelism.

Training in evangelism	Rapid change in culture; most evangelizers unprepared.
Confidence in witness	Christians are isolated, angry, and fearful toward many non-Christians. Christians have been led to believe that non-Christians have rejected the gospel or are uninterested. Result: defensive posture; loss of confidence that God can use us in evangelism.
Commitment to the Great Commission	Little emphasis on evangelism, especially in contrast to other Christian and secular concerns.
Ready to go	Attack on health, funds, personal lives, and marriages of those dedicated to evangelism.
Clear on basic doctrines	Teaching on universalism (all will be saved); anti-consequence (there is no hell).
Task of Christians	Redefined away from evangelism.

I believe one reason for this crisis in evangelism is that Satan has masterminded a megastrategy to stop evangelism. There are attacks on believers, non-Christians, the character of God, the gospel message . . . you name it. Satan has hit so many things at once that we are reeling with confusion.

Another reason for this crisis is that we've lost the meaning of the word "love." *Agape* love (God's kind of love) affirms, supports, holds up, helps, exhorts, and brings healing. Jesus accepted people where they were, then helped them become what they could become. His love, as our love should, helped people become open to the Holy Spirit of God who can convict and lead to truth.[1]

A third reason is that we've lost a first-century perspective. What if Jesus looked at our evangelism?

Would he wonder why we don't bother to discuss the issues of life and death with a next-door neighbor? Would he wonder why we retreat to the comfortable suburbs, leaving our cities in pain and without a witness? Would he be concerned about the vying for power and position, the jealousy and intolerance among those who profess to be dedicated to the Great Commission? Or would he be grieved by the immorality and greed among those who are to lead the flock in evangelism? Would he wonder why the church is so angry, fearful, and frustrated when he has called us to love and has provided for our needs? Would he ask us why we don't read his Word afresh to drive out confusion and paralysis?

I am disturbed, as many are, that the social and cultural environment is not what we would like. Only last year someone broke into my home, threatening with a knife. I have been in hotel chains where the pornography offered in each room creates a pervasive atmosphere of lust and leering at the women in the lobbies and common areas. I have hated it when the grocery store in my community displayed pornographic magazines at the check-out stand. (In fact, I asked them to please remove the magazines and they did.) I feel uncomfortable with the pressure to accept men walking hand-in-hand with men. I love what other women have done to help elevate women, insisting on more pay and better positions, but I cringe when I learn that some radical groups are encouraging women to worship strange deities. New-Age thought troubles me because adherents are deceived about the effects of ungrounded and unstable ideas on a life and culture.

In the seventies I wrote newsletter columns encouraging honorable citizens to rise up and be heard in the social context. But I never would have imagined that the result of social awareness and political activism would be a generation of angry and fearful Christians who have allowed the intensity of this battle to strip them of their God-given *agape* love for the lost individual and rob them of their vision for evangelism.

Have all non-Christians made *conscious* choices to defy God? Are they necessarily and overtly anti-God and out to destroy us—or have sloppy thinking and unexamined prejudices about life distorted our perceptions? Has the Western style of putting everyone in a box, categorizing, and organizing backfired? Has it kept us from seeing unbelievers as God sees them—souls in need of his love and grace and truth? Have we opted for the easier route of putting everyone in categories so we don't have to do the work of finding out where they are and what our responsibility is to them?

What would we do if we found out that some are prepared to receive God's Good News? What if we learned that some have been listening to the still small voice but have been hindered by believers who have neglected or garbled God's summons?

We forget that nonbelievers are blinded by Satan and are enslaved by sin, just as we were before we heard the gospel and received salvation. What we fail to acknowledge is that many of us still act that way even after salvation.

Meanwhile, the non-Christian watches us, wondering why we are doing what we are doing. Ben, a bright twelve-year-old, is an unchurched youngster in my neighborhood whom I befriended little by little. He went with me to a Memorial Day picnic at a nearby church. Karyn, another twelve-year-old neighbor who is a new Christian, also went along. The two of them roamed the church and found a door marked Prayer Room. Karyn entered. Ben resisted.

"Come on," she said. Ben refused again, obviously shaken.

"Why won't you come in?" Karyn asked.

"Do I have to pray?" asked Ben.

"No, of course not."

Still Ben, who has no knowledge about God and who has never prayed, would not enter, frightened at the prospect of a God and the idea of addressing him.

Throughout the world there are adults who are very like Ben. They shrink from encounters with the Almighty and feel he has no relevance for their lives. They may be alcoholics or crafty lawyers or radical cultish leaders. They may be journalists without an understanding of the spiritual, or university professors who shield their fear of the Almighty by taking a view opposing religion, or actors seeking a name for themselves and negatively influencing the next generation. They cannot understand the kindness of God and the life he wishes to impart, nor do they have the knowledge of God's holiness and their own lostness. They need someone to tell them. Are we willing?

Note

1. Jesus' meaning of love is demonstrated in these stories: the Good Samaritan (Luke 10:33); the title "Daughter of Abraham" (Luke 13:16) with which he addressed a woman; his invitation to the children to come to him (Mark 10:13); the forgiveness offered the adulterous woman (John 8: 1-11); and his actions toward the woman healed of the issue of blood (Luke 8:43-44).

Chapter Two

We Are Not Little Gods

A hairdresser was often crass and vulgar and this disturbed some of his Christian clientele. One Christian customer, Carla,[1] decided not to be subjected to this behavior, so she took her business elsewhere. Later she learned that her former hairdresser had become a Christian. Carla returned and confessed to him why she had left and how offended she had been at his behavior. He replied, "Jesus was never offended. You should have remained my customer and prayed for me. Why didn't you tell me about the love of Christ?"

I'm sorry to report that this self-righteous attitude toward non-Christians is not uncommon. Just last week I heard about another Christian who I'll call Debbie who telephoned a non-Christian female acquaintance to tell her that because she slept with her boyfriend, Debbie would no longer be able to carry on a friendship. The friend was hurt deeply and ended up feeling rejected by God.

Those who agree with such actions claim they are following Christ, but are they? To answer that question, let's take a closer look at Jesus and Paul, our models for how to relate to nonbelievers. Jesus and Paul blazed the trail for how to teach the Word of God. They, too, confronted ignorance and disbelief, but one thing is clear: They did not treat the immoral, the misinformed, the tax collector, or the politician as the enemy.

Carla and Debbie had forgotten two clear tenets of Scripture: We are to love and reach out to the unbeliever and we are not to judge outsiders. Paul wrote:

> I have written you in my letter not to associate with sexually immoral people—not at all meaning the people of this world who are immoral, or the greedy and swindlers, or idolaters. In that case you would have to leave this world. What business is it of mine to judge those outside the church? Are you not to judge those inside? God will judge those outside (1 Corinthians 5:9-13).

According to Luke:

> Now the tax collectors and "sinners" [or maybe we should say abortionists, mystics, New-Agers, homosexuals, adulterers, prostitutes, thieves, secular humanists, corrupt politicians, and journalists] were all gathering around to hear him [Jesus] (Luke 15:1).

If Jesus walked our streets, what would be the first thing that would grip him? Immorality? Greed? Would he rail at the vice and condemn those who didn't worship God? Would he shake his finger or hurl his fists at liberals and journalists because they have another viewpoint than some of his children? Actually Jesus, while he walked the streets of Palestine, scolded people like us who misrepresented him to the masses.

How Jesus Saw People

Jesus, understanding the diversity and complexities of human nature, condemned the religious leaders for their misuse of Scripture and God's temple. He railed at them for misrepresenting God's character and heaving unnecessary burdens on people. But his treatment of publicans and sinners was quite different. He dined with them! He went to where they were, in their arenas, and didn't wait for them to come hear him speak in a synagogue.

Jesus said that love, even for the unlovely, corrupt, and far out, was the greatest commandment and that love's practice fulfilled all his law. This he practiced continually.

Some might ask, did Jesus realize what he was doing? Was he naive about his listeners? Did Jesus not recognize that this odious crowd was the enemy, hurting his people and wrecking their cities? Why else would he waste his time bringing them a chance at eternal and abundant life? It's clear from the text that Jesus did know what he was doing and he understood how it went against the teaching of the religious leaders of the day. Let's take a closer look at several of Jesus' encounters with people of questionable character.

Most Jews scorned tax collectors, but Jesus entered the home of one, Zacchaeus, and talked with him about his sin and need of a better way of living.

"Zacchaeus, come down immediately. I must stay at your house today." All the people saw this and began to mutter, "He has gone to be the guest of a 'sinner.'"

But Zacchaeus stood up and said to the Lord, "Look, Lord! Here and now I give half of my possessions to the poor, and if I have cheated anybody out of anything, I will pay back four times the amount." Jesus said to him, "Today salvation has come to this house" (Luke 19:5,7-9).

In another instance Jesus was invited to dinner at the home of Simon the Pharisee. A prostitute heard Jesus was there and came to the house with some expensive perfume and knelt down before him, weeping, and wiped his feet with the perfume. Simon was offended that Jesus would allow this sinner to touch him. But Jesus disagreed, saying,

Do you see this woman? I came into your house. You did not give me any water for my feet, but she wet my feet with her tears and wiped them with her hair. You did not give me a kiss, but this woman from the time I entered, has not stopped kissing my feet. You did not put oil on my head, but she has poured perfume on my feet. Therefore, I tell you, her many sins have been forgiven (Luke 7:44-47).

Jesus didn't doom her or avoid contact with her. He saw her as an individual and looked at her heart.

In yet another example, Jesus encountered a Samaritan woman who had married five times and was living with a man. She would have not been eligible to be held up as a model for a pro-family agenda today, but she *was* qualified for the Good News.

So he [Jesus] came to a town in Samaria called Sychar, near the plot of ground Jacob had given to his son Joseph. Jacob's well was there, and Jesus, tired as he was from the journey, sat down by the well. It was about the sixth hour.

When a Samaritan came to draw water, Jesus said to

her, "Will you give me a drink?" (His disciples had gone into the town to buy food.)

The Samaritan woman said to him, "You are a Jew and I am a Samaritan woman. How can you ask me for a drink?" (For Jews do not associate with Samaritans.)

Jesus answered her, "If you knew the gift of God and who it is that asks you for a drink, you would have asked him and he would have given you living water."

"Sir," the woman said, "you have nothing to draw with and the well is deep. Where can you get this living water? Are you greater than our father Jacob, who gave us the well and drank from it himself, as did also his sons and his flocks and herds?"

Jesus answered and said to her, "Everyone who drinks this water will be thirsty again, but whoever drinks the water I give him will never thirst. Indeed, the water I give him will become in him a spring of water welling up to eternal life."

The woman said to him, "Sir, give me this water so I won't get thirsty and have to keep coming here to draw water."

He told her, "Go, call your husband and come back."

"I have no husband," she replied.

Jesus said to her, "You are right when you say you have no husband. The fact is, you have had five husbands, and the man you now have is not your husband. What you have just said is quite true."

"Sir," the woman said, "I can see that you are a prophet. Our fathers worshiped on this mountain, but you Jews claim that the place where we must worship is in Jerusalem."

Jesus declared, "Believe me, woman, a time is coming when you will worship the Father neither on this mountain nor in Jerusalem. You Samaritans worship what you do not know; we worship what we do know, for salvation is from the Jews. Yet a time is coming and has now come when the true worshipers will worship the Father in spirit and truth, for they are the kind of worshipers the Father seeks. God is spirit, his worshipers must worship in spirit and in truth."

The woman said, "I know that Messiah" (called Christ) "is coming. When he comes, He will explain everything to us."

Then Jesus declared, "I who speak to you am he."

Just then his disciples returned and were surprised to find him talking with a woman. But no one asked, "What do You want?" or "Why are you talking with her?"

Then, leaving her water jar, the woman went back to the town and said to the people, "Come, see a man who told me everything I ever did. Could this be the Christ?" They came out of the town and made their way toward him.

Many of the Samaritans from that town believed in him because of the woman's testimony, "He told me everything I ever did" (John 4:1-30,39).

The official Jewish position on Samaritans was judgmental. They categorized and labeled Gentiles as especially unclean and unfit for contact. The Samaritan woman's behavior (had she produced children?) would have contributed to the breakdown of the family and the tumbling of morals in society. But Jesus did not talk with her about changing her lifestyle for the sake of her country or focus on how she had weakened the fiber of society. Instead, he gained the woman's attention, aroused her curiosity, and let her know that he knew and cared about her life. He then offered her "living water" to sustain her and wash away her sin.

I wonder how she would have felt and responded if Jesus had talked with her about ethics rather than quenching her thirst? If he had told her to get her life straightened out rather than offering her a Messiah and a Savior?

Are We Like Jesus?

Jesus reached out to those whom much of the church condemns today. "I have not come to call the righteous," Jesus pleaded, "but sinners to repentance" (Luke 5:32). They, in turn, yearned to know what Jesus had to say. However, the religious leaders of Jesus' day challenged Jesus' actions, as if these people were less worthy and desirous of hearing and acting upon his message. Are we guilty of the same?

What do we think about being a loving witness to a pro-choice individual or a homosexual or a feminist? If we are to follow Christ's example and commands, we have no choice but to go to them, offering the gospel with a heart of benevolence—even if we believe they abhor God. God takes no delight in the punishment of the wicked (see Ezekiel 33:11). We are to show the world the heart of God because "Christ's love compels us" (2 Corinthians 5:14) and because it is a direct command of Christ (see Matthew 28:19-20). Either we are obedient to Christ's command to reach the world—the whole world—or we need to admit our disobedience. Either our actions show we agree with the Father that none should perish (see 2 Peter 3:9) or they indicate we have created a theology of disobedience.

Called to Be a Light

Paul gives us another example of how to evangelize. While the Roman empire was persecuting and killing Christians, he demonstrated adept understanding of God, humans, and the gospel as he stood before Agrippa.

Then Agrippa said to Paul, "You have permission to speak for yourself."

So Paul motioned with his hand and began his defense: "King Agrippa, I consider myself fortunate to stand before you today as I make my defense against all the accusations of the Jews, and especially so because you are well acquainted with all the Jewish customs and controversies. Therefore, I beg you to listen to me patiently.". . . At this point Festus interrupted Paul's defense. "You are out of your mind, Paul!" he shouted. "Your great learning is driving you insane."

"I am not insane, most excellent Festus," Paul replied (Acts 26:1-3,24-25).

Notice how Paul was not arrogant or offensive. He treated the king and Festus with respect and honor. Of course, Paul was arguing for his life. It was in his best interest not to add to his charges. But still, he wanted a hearing amid the philosophical hurdles, bumps, and obstacles. Note, he did not try to change the moral status of the empire, nor did he argue for the protection of Christians, though this type of emphasis is entirely appropriate and supported by Scripture.

Similar to the way Paul addressed Roman politicians is his approach to the day's philosophers.

While Paul was waiting for them in Athens, he was greatly distressed to see that the city was full of idols. So he reasoned in the synagogue with the Jews and the God-fearing Greeks, as well as in the marketplace day by day with those who happened to be there. A group of Epicurean and Stoic philosophers began to dispute with him. Some of them asked, "What is this babbler trying to say?" Others remarked, "He seems to be advocating foreign gods." They said this because Paul was preaching the good news about Jesus and the resurrection. Then they took him and brought him to a meeting of the Areopagus, where they said to him, "May we know what this new teaching is that you are presenting? You are bringing some strange ideas to our ears, and we want to know what they mean." (All the Athenians and the foreigners who lived there spent their time doing nothing but talking about and listening to the latest ideas.)

Paul then stood up in the meeting of the Areopagus and said, "Men of Athens! I see that in every way you are very religious. For as I walked around and looked carefully at your objects of worship, I even found an altar with this inscription: TO AN UNKNOWN GOD. Now what you worship as something unknown I am going to proclaim to you. The God who made the world and everything in it is the Lord of heaven and earth and does not live in temples built by hands. And he is not served by human hands, as if he needed anything, because he himself gives all men life and breath and everything else. From one man he made every nation of men, that they should inhabit the whole earth; and he determined the times set for them and the exact places where they should live. God did this so that men would seek him and perhaps reach out for him and find him, though he is not far from each one of us. For in Him we live and move and have our being. As some of your own poets have said, "We are his offspring" (Acts 17:16-28).

At the Areopagus Paul neither censured nor denounced the worldly philosophers. There were no reproofs of how they were leading others astray by incorrect and unbiblical ideas. Instead, he saw their point of view as a stepping stone, a bridge to the gospel. He acknowledged their interest in philosophical matters, and referred to their altar "to the unknown god." He quoted one of their own poets to artfully open the conversation about Christ and then challenge them that they needed to turn from idols to the true God.

Do we care enough to listen, love, and tell philosophers, professors, and those engaged in cults that they're perhaps on the right train (seeking meaning) but on the wrong track?

Paul's attempts to reach the unbeliever where they were in keeping with his call. God's word to Paul had been: "I have made you a light for the Gentiles, that you may bring salvation to the ends of the earth" (Acts 13:47). This call to be a light is the call to all believers throughout the New Testament. As Jesus said, "God did not send his Son into the world to condemn the world, but to save the world through Him" (John 3:17). The Proverbs declare, we are to *rescue* those who are perishing (Proverbs 24:11). Paul's attitude toward these non-Christians in Athens reflected biblical principles: Love believes the best (see 1 Corinthians 13); show respect to all people (see 1 Peter 2:17); and make the most of every opportunity (Ephesians 5:16).

We Are Not Little Gods

Those who don't know God will often avoid anything that smacks of bigoted narrow mindedness. He or she chooses another path rather than being identified with intolerance, ungraciousness, or judgmentalism—which sadly describes many Christians today.

If that sounds harsh, it is; but it needs to be said. At times, we have become what we despise. We accuse the non-Christian of being intolerant and ungenerous toward us, but we have learned to be so toward them, using harsh labels and categorizing. We sow frustration, partiality, and resentment, but expect to reap understanding, grace, and love.

Several years ago the *Washington Post* had an article describing Christians as uneducated and easily led. Pat Robertson rightly challenged them on the misrepresentation, but have we not ever done the same to the unchurched?

Oddly, Christians and secularists are playing a similar game with one another. Each is entrenched in a fight to determine which way the country will go and both often forget the people involved. The secularists are seeking a humanistic utopia and desire the good of the world. However, they fail to realize the world will only be truly changed when placed under God's rule. As Christ taught us to pray, "Your kingdom come, your will be done on earth as it is in heaven" (Matthew 6:9-10).

Christians, on the other hand, though they have the truth of the gospel, often get in the way of the gospel. We forget that the people who have a right—no, more than that, an eternal right—to hear the gospel have varying points of view, interests, and backgrounds. They are *real* persons with circumstances that indeed affect their thinking, behavior, and choices.

Like Jesus and Paul we need to approach people with generous hearts and believe the best about the motives of those with whom we disagree. We can communicate that:

- the person with whom we are talking wishes to make the best decisions for his or her life;

- many women adopt a feminist point of view simply because they want equal pay and equal respect;

- the secular press seeks to give a fair story;

- the liberals are sincerely seeking to help their country;

- New-Agers are looking for answers and also experience inner voids;

- secular humanists are seeking to define life to make sense to themselves;

- many film makers think in terms of artistry and many do not grapple with deeper meaning or the reasons behind them.

Our first encounter with people who view things differently than us should be respectful. We should offer them the benefit of the doubt. If you were in their shoes, how would you like to be treated? Isn't this what Jesus' "golden rule" is all about?

In order to treat others as we would like to be treated and to communicate the gospel effectively, we need to understand how the non-Christian sees us. That's the subject of the next chapter. Many Christians believe there is "no hope for our world." They don't witness at work because "no one is interested." They isolate themselves to church and home in order to protect their children. Fear, anger, and discouragement dominate their perspective. Sadly, such a mindset validates the non-Christian's perspective.

We, of all people, are not to be afraid or angry or defeated or isolated. What, then, should be our perspective?

Note

1. A few names in this book have been changed to respect anonymity.

Chapter Three

How Do Non-Christians See Us?

I often drive a busy freeway between my home and my parents' home. Along with thousands of other drivers I observe a prominent Christian sign. For several years the sign warned against abortion. Then the sign urged families to pray. On one trip I saw that something truly significant must have happened to the property owners. The sign read in huge letters, "THANK YOU, JESUS."

I am heartened when I pass that plot because I know that fellow Christians who love the Lord live there. But always in the back of my mind I am wondering, "What do non-Christians think when they read this sign or the other signs that Christians erect? Do these signs inspire unbelievers to consider God? Do they make them wonder about the strange behavior of the owners? Do our messages confuse others? Do our messages make people feel uncomfortable and repelled? What about the signs we project as individuals to a non-believing world through words, body language, and attitudes? Do these "signs" represent the sacrificial love of Jesus, or are they simply ways to salve our consciences, or project to other Christians that we are "good" Christians?

Like countless other Christians, I am gripped by the reality of heaven and hell and I long to see people won to Christ. I struggle with communicating the gospel in a way people can understand and I plead with God for the lives of others. I search faces as I make my daily rounds wondering, "Do they know God?" "What are they thinking about?" "What barriers are keeping them from thinking about their own destiny?" "What would it take to get them to consider Christ, to be open to the loving and forgiving Jesus?"

Of course social action has its time and place, and is needed today. Ethics and principles are important in a society and to work for their implementation is commendable. It is right for one to defend one's country, to make it better, to do things for the betterment of all. But is this all we're doing?

I believe if a poll were taken among non-Christians only a fraction of those interviewed could accurately relate what a Christian is and how to become a Christian.[1] Not only is the meaning of the gospel misunderstood; we Christians have lost our reputation as caring people. The unconverted suspect our motives and agenda, and their sometimes accurate perceptions of us have created a barrier which prevents them from hearing the true gospel message.

Attempts to Control

One of these perceptions is that Christians are out to control everyone's behavior. Many of us act as if we are parents and non-Christians are teenagers needing direction, instruction, and even control. Naturally the unbeliever resents any attempt of Christians to control their behavior. The Bible, for good reason, tells us to take the back seat at the banquet, then perhaps the host will honor us with a seat up front. We need to apply this truth to our evangelistic endeavors. Few of us, if any, like someone treading on what we consider our territory. So if Christians want to gain a hearing in the world, we must not barge in as if we belong in the front row and as if we have all the answers. Such behavior is offensive and builds barriers.

We need to thoughtfully and prayerfully make opportunity for the gospel. I was shopping recently at a mall. As I left the drug store a young man in his early thirties made eye contact with me. As he was passing he smiled and said hello. I returned his smile and said hello as I continued toward my car.

Suddenly he backed up and looked me in the eye. "Do you know Jesus loves you?" I had had a very tough week and was fumbling in my assurance of God's love for me at the moment. "Yes, I do," I answered.

He shifted feet and sought to make eye contact again. "Do you know that Jesus died and was brought back to life for you?" he asked as he now commanded the sidewalk in conversation. I wanted to affirm that I was a Christian but also wanted to know what he might say, so I responded, "Yes, I do."

"Then live in hope!" he said, watching my response to see if I received his message. Assured that I had heard him he then entered the store.

My spirits soared with the simple reminder of where my hope lies and of God's love for me. This man's urgency was founded in love. There wasn't a question in my mind that the Holy Spirit had prompted his remarks because the Spirit bore witness inside of me.

In contrast to this, many Christians today often try to control others—and as a result experience resistance. Most people do not wish to be told what to do, to be coerced, maneuvered, and so lose the right of decision making. When talking to people about our beliefs, we need to acknowledge, "It is your life, not mine. I respect your right to make whatever decision you choose. My interest is to communicate information to you for your consideration. There are reasons why I feel as I do that have made a big difference in my own life. May I share them with you?"

Learning to Listen

Another perception non-Christians have of Christians is that we are only interested in our own agenda and opinions. We aren't willing to listen to other people's viewpoints.

Several years ago I realized I needed to start listening to non-Christians more keenly. I decided to survey non-Christians of various viewpoints in order to better understand human nature and the reasons people make choices. I visited a secular bookstore where I had seen an Indian religion seminar announcement tacked up by the side of the door. Linda, one of the ladies in the bookstore, was setting up the seminar. I introduced myself as a writer, explaining that I was seeking interviews to determine how people felt and thought about what they believe. Would she be willing to give me an honest interview?

She agreed. A few days later we met and for the first hour I asked her questions such as:

Why do you think you are alive?
Who do you think you are and why?
What does the idea of "spirituality" suggest to you?

What do you think of when you hear the words "life" or "death"?

Who is God in your estimation? What do you think or feel when you consider God?

Do you experience guilt?

How can you be sure you are headed in the right direction?

On what basis do you make decisions?

What are you afraid of? How do you overcome fear?

What has your background contributed to your understanding about life?

What do you believe about life and why?

Do you believe in good and evil?

I also asked, "Have you had a spiritual journey you would like to share?" Linda excitedly told me of her spiritual guide and how this being had instructed her. She thought this guide was a good being and cited ways she felt she had been helped. Even though I desired to help her understand the danger of such a "guide," I did not challenge her, knowing it would shut down the conversation prematurely.

Two hours into the conversation I asked Linda what she thought of Jesus. She said he was a great white light. I suggested that her response made me curious. Some, I told her, suggest that Jesus is a good person; some a little god; some a prophet; others said he was not important to consider. It seemed unfair to me, I said, that people made Jesus what they wanted him to be. "If people defined you any way they wanted, tailoring you for their convenience, how would that make you feel?" I asked politely. She seemed to think about this and we continued.

As the survey drew to a conclusion I asked her if she would be willing to read a book about Christianity. "Considering your background, it would be very interesting to get your response," I told her. The conversation opened up a bit more into a Christian direction. Finally Linda said to me, "You know, I think you're supposed to be here today. All of my life I have tried to find myself and somehow I believe now I am supposed to try to find God. I have been thinking about this."

My conversation with Linda reminded me that had I not asked questions and listened I would not have had the slightest idea that she had thought about knowing God. It also reminded me that labels can limit our ability to accurately perceive what an individual really is and believes. It also showed me that a non-controlling, listening stance created the opportunity for Linda to tell the truth about herself so that the gospel could eventually be presented.

I realize that I don't have all the answers about life. I have been a Christian for a number of decades, yet there is much I do not know. At times God and life baffle me. I say this in the context of having spent years in Bible study, having done graduate work in theology, and having spent many years in Christian work. Why should I approach Linda as if she has nothing to contribute to my understanding about human need and life's dilemmas? What Christian, just by virtue of praying a prayer to receive Christ, has the corner on all truth? Understanding myself, being sensitive to the Holy Spirit, and listening to Linda were vital to connecting to this dear woman.

Behind the Times?

Many non-Christians see Christians as misguided and behind the times. They feel we are unloving and often disdainful toward their lifestyles, their decisions, and the way they are running their lives.

What Christians often fail to acknowledge is that many who do not know Christ are making choices for their lives as best they can. When they hurt they look for a way to stop hurting. They know nothing of God's healing balm so they create protective defensive patterns of response should hurt come again. They feel shame. And because they know nothing of Jesus and his sacrifice on the cross, they pick up a current how-to psychology book to find a way to handle their shame. At each turn in their lives they manage without God's help.

What do we do when they are at our door? Will we seek to listen and connect? Will we remember our past and be honest about our own foolish decisions and open our hearts and hopes to them? Will we feel safe enough in God's love that we can share our own pains, hidden hungers and hopes so we can connect with them and share the answers we have found?

Many non-Christians know they fail at being the perfect woman and the perfect man. They are not successful or wealthy or intellectual. They feel unacceptable. Like us, they have frustrations of everyday life, yet with no One to turn to for help. Most of them have discovered that it's better to play along, to pretend they're something that they're not, to take second-rate answers, than to face the possibility of seeking honest solutions and finding there are none. They are, as Jesus said, "sheep without a shepherd" and need an opportunity to make a U-turn and come home.

Are we Christians able to meet them where they are? Or are our vocabulary and metaphors behind the times? I suspect they are. "Shout it from the rooftops," we sing, yet houses today are not built with platforms that can be used for speaking as they were in biblical (and other) times. We say, "You need to be redeemed" but the average person doesn't understand the reference being made to slave markets.

What would happen to our attempts to evangelize if our songs and sermons reflected this generation? For example, let's have a song that says, "Tell it at the mall, the playground, inside the hospitals and jails, and outside the psychiatric clinics." We don't normally have a market square, but we have street corners and beaches, office buildings, neighborhood barbecues, and community pools. Why not tell people they can be free as hostages from captivity or prisoners of war from lengthy internment?

Maybe we are seen as misguided and behind the times because we are. If we spent more time around non-Christians, maybe we'd come to understand them better and be able to identify their struggles. I'm thankful that some Christians today are doing this. They are at the jail, the hospital, the bar, the university classroom, the club, the gym, neighborhood parties, PTA meetings, and rehabilitation clinics, seeking to hold out the light in a relevant and contemporary style.

Think for Yourself!

Non-Christians also accuse Christians of having a pack mentality. There is a reason for this. It's rare to hear us acknowledge that while we believe in some non-negotiables, the Christian community has different viewpoints on negotiable subjects. Rarely do we publicly affirm that God allows variety and that diversity can be healthy, as long as it is guided by Scripture.

It is much more common to hear one Christian's opinion as being the "Christian" perspective. A recent issue of *Redbook* had an article on condoms which indicated that the "religious right's" viewpoint was anti-condom. In reality there is a difference of opinion in the Christian community on the use of condoms and many other issues: prayer in schools, women's rights and roles, alternative health care, and abortion, to name a few. And look at the divergent views on doctrine.

When Christians are seen as a pack, it looks like we are uneducated, unthinking, unaware of individual conscience. We appear to be people who follow unthinkingly the popular Christian party line. There is a Christian "party line"— the mind of Christ. However, we must be careful not to insist that our particular position on a contemporary issue is absolute Christian truth for all time and all people. Some humility is called for.

The Bible speaks of absolute truth, but it also speaks of individual conscience. For example, it talks about whether a Christian should eat meat offered to idols, a hot issue to the first-century Christian. Interestingly the conclusion is neither yes nor no, but an appeal to personal conscience, offering a wide berth for Christians to make up their own minds. "Be careful, however, that the exercise of your freedom does not become a stumbling block to the weak" (1 Corinthians 8:9; also see 1 Corinthians 8-9). We would do well to remember this, especially when speaking to non-Christians about what Christians believe.

When we speak to others we should emphasize that we do not speak for *all* Christians on issues. Christians, in fact, have individual consciences and viewpoints and styles of expression. Indeed our most mature leaders sometimes disagree with one another. Witness, for example, Paul and Barnabas, Acts 15:

> And after some days Paul said to Barnabas, "Come, let us return and visit the brethren in every city where we proclaimed the word of the Lord, and see how they are. And Barnabas wanted to take with them John called Mark. But Paul thought best not to take with them one who had withdrawn from them in

Pamphylia, and had not gone with them to the work. And there arose a sharp contention, so that they separated from each other . . . (Acts 15:36-39, RSV).

Even though in the same chapter Paul and Barnabas were united on some doctrinal issues being decided by the church at large, they obviously disagreed on a significant practical matter—whether Mark should travel with them. When appropriate we should emphasize that Christians make individual choices on a variety of subjects, and that individual conscience on these issues within the broad boundaries of Scripture is respected in the Christian camp.

If one looks at history, and particularly church history, we see how strategic this advice is. In every generation, church leaders have fought over various issues. Often Satan has used these disputes to alienate seekers. Even as recently as forty years ago, many refused to consider the claims of Christ lest they be taken from pleasures they enjoyed—smoking, drinking, card playing, and dancing. These behaviors were often equated with salvation by the non-Christian, yet none of these activities are given as standards in the Bible by which to judge whether we are or are not saved.

Not only can it be argued that Christians sometimes follow leaders indiscriminately, but many Christians don't think critically or reflectively. Reflective thought indicates that a cognitive process is taking place concerning the meaning and application of the material being presented. Critical thought, which is the ability to think logically, analytically, and conclusively, is important in coming to unbiased truth. C. S. Lewis appealed to people's ability to think critically when he presented the "trilemma" argument. He proposed that Jesus was either a liar, a lunatic, or Lord. He went on to disprove that Jesus is a liar or lunatic and thus concluded that one can assume Jesus is the Lord.

The logical argument still fares well among the educated.

Good communication does not simply play on emotions to get a response. A pastor who had become involved in the pro-life movement was asked to speak at a pro-life rally. As was his habit, he prepared a convincing talk, utilizing Scripture, logic, and reason. The speakers who preceded him and followed him, he noted, were not presenting substance. Their presentations lacked intellectual integrity. They would toss out particular phrases and the audience came alive.

The pastor decided to try this style for himself. On his second time up to the platform, he raised his voice and said, "Let's not give the devil a victory." The audience cheered.

"They're killing the next generation." Again the crowd voiced their applause. "These lives will never see God's creation." This, too, was met with applause.

Though we don't like to admit it, many in the American church have become empty listeners, responding mindlessly to select phrases and input. This is a tragedy! Every believer would benefit from a study of logic and communication as well as a mastery of the Bible in order to accurately judge truth.

Is Morality a Substitute for the Gospel?

Many non-Christians, if asked, would define the Christian as a moralist. They believe that to be a Christian is to be antiabortion, antigay, etc.

What is it that we are asking of nonbelievers? Are we saying, "Be moral so I'll feel better"? Are we demanding that the unregenerate person behave like a Christian? I heard a report a few years back in the Christian media about the Rodney King trial in Southern California.

Rodney King, a black motorist, was severely beaten by the police who apprehended him. The beating, captured on videotape, sparked controversial trials, wide media coverage, and tragic riots. The report told of a letter being sent to the president of the United States declaring that Los Angeles needed a reinstatement of morals. Nothing was mentioned about the urgency of evangelism.

I was puzzled. Do people in Watts (South Central Los Angeles) not know that killing is wrong? Do they not understand that stealing is wrong and that harassing ethnic groups is wrong? If we describe the appropriate standards and tell people "You need to shape up," will they?

Obviously, this is not the case. We have forgotten humankind has always acted selfishly and destructively, despite the presence of moral values. History tells us that. For example, look at the slaughter that occurred in America during the Civil War or the licentiousness of the roaring twenties. During the early years of this country there was vast pilfering, thievery, prostitution, alcoholism, drug use, and political murder. Are we that naive or uneducated in history?

Undoubtedly, our children and young people *should* be taught the basics of decency as well as the ABCs. Respect for authority, respect for property, and respect for the rights of others should be drilled into youth right alongside reading and arithmetic. Watching out for one's neighbor and minding our business in ways that do not hurt others should be taught and valued. Respect for human dignity and love for one another should be reinforced year after year in history, sociology, political science, literature, and other classes, as well as in the churches and the homes.

When we are attempting to persuade the leaders of our culture to promote decency, honor, and love, we need to be wise. Good-natured humor, repartee, and the use of irony when mixed with good reasoning may win an opponent to our side. Sometimes we need to be firm and expose potentially harmful viewpoints as impractical, inconsistent, and unworkable. We need to use logical arguments freely, comparing, contrasting, and describing. However, we should avoid using overstatement and generalizations.

At times it will be necessary, even expedient, to get tough and refuse inordinate compromise. But such confrontation should be used only if our cause clearly has the blessings of Almighty God. Otherwise we may find we are working against the purposes of God. We need God's help and wisdom in these matters.

As I watched the television report on South Central Los Angeles, I thought back to my days at the World Christian Training Center in Watts. At that time (in the 1970s) Christians were praying en masse for their city. More than 140 South Central Los Angeles churches had some members involved in a witnessing program. Correspondingly, crime went down. Community relations improved. With the Good News presentation people had come face-to-face with the realization of God's love and their own sins. First came a change of heart; then a change in viewpoint; then a change in behavior. When the World Christian Training Center died and evangelism went on the back burner in the minds and hearts of South Central Christians, the area slowly went back to havoc despite social programs, a concerned board of education, and worried parents.

We know that the law is God's tool to lead us to Christ and that no society can function successfully without moral norms and standards. *But* if we think that reestablishing morals in our country, apart from the gospel, will produce the land we desire, we, as Christians, have moved right off the board.

Do We Care?

The unchurched often feel that the church is not enriching, peaceful, and joyful. What are they faced with when they visit most churches? Do people say hello? Do they care?

Do we create an environment where God is and where he can be reflected? What else would make people desire our message? We are, the Bible tells us, God's message to the world. You and I! Therefore we need to be Christlike by offering unconditional, loving acceptance, and by being real, transparent persons who admit when we are wrong and are careful to convey we do not have all the answers. But we must also give the message of eternal life and be sensitive to the Holy Spirit and obedient to his leadership. A welcoming approach and emphasis helps to overcome mistrust and defensiveness.

In conclusion, let me point out that social and lifestyle issues must be evaluated prayerfully. What we decide to fight for and the way we choose to fight become part of the gospel environment we create.

Note

1. See George Barna, *What Christians Believe*.

Chapter Four

Who Is This Contemporary Non-Christian?

I f we misunderstand people, we will most likely miscommunicate with them. Common sense tells us that we must properly assess ourselves and others or our communication will break down. If we don't understand what the Bible says about how a person is made and how that works out spiritually between a person and God, our evangelism will not be effective.

For many years I have had the privilege of traveling worldwide to advise Christian leaders on the means of communicating the gospel to their cultures. I have observed firsthand that no matter what the human variables, the gospel fits every person in the world. People are essentially the same the world over and from generation to generation. Our fallen human natures need divine help. Part of our task as evangelizers is learning who our audience is and what they need and desire. If we don't understand them, we won't be able to help them see how the gospel affects them.

Primary Identity

Who *is* the non-Christian? The non-Christian, who bears the image of God, whether female or male, young or old, thin or heavy, black, brown, yellow, or white, is an individual for whom Christ's death and resurrection can have temporal and eternal consequences. "He is the atoning sacrifice for our sins, and not only for ours but also for the sins of the whole world" (1 John 2:2).

Every person is a complex mixture of temperament, heritage, and environmental influences. All individuals are made with a need for God, a need for giving and receiving love, for significance, for meaning and purpose, for forgiveness, and for hope for the future. This is touching the barest foundations of human makeup. Every person is an amalgamation of input from parents, teachers, neighbors, friends, enemies, books they have read, movies they have seen, and demonic influences to which they have been subjected. We are all individuals whom God has formed and whom the world, the flesh, and the Devil have fashioned. Each of us is different and evangelizers must not make the mistake of stereotyping or generalizing.

Many evangelistic organizations speak of evangelism in terms of people groups in order to make manageable the worldwide, countrywide, and citywide tasks and to discern cultural tendencies. But when it comes to personal intercession and evangelism, we need to think in terms of individuals. This characterizes a major difference between an "issue stance" and a "gospel stance." An issue stance uses grouping and labeling to make a point while a gospel stance sees each separate, individual person as one for whom Christ died. God absolutely does not give us the prerogative to make up our minds ahead of time as to who will receive or who will reject His substitutionary death—no matter what they believe or what they do or have done. Every person's truest identity is that they are made in the image of God and are someone for whom Christ died.

Influenced by the Evil One

Satan dominates and influences the unconverted person. Paul tells us that those who were formerly unsaved were led by disobedient spirits (Ephesians 2:2). The Bible tells us that Satan "has blinded the minds of unbelievers, so that they cannot see the light of the gospel of the glory of Christ, who is the image of God" (2 Corinthians 4:4). Paul then follows this statement by saying, "For God, who said, 'Let light shine out of darkness,' made his light shine in our hearts to give us the light of the knowledge of the glory of God in the face of Christ" (2 Corinthians 4:6). Luke, writing of Paul's testimony before Agrippa, pens, "I am sending you to them to open their eyes and turn them from darkness to light, and from the power of Satan to God, so that they may receive forgiveness of sins . . ." (Acts 26:17-18).

Even though we do not have complete knowledge about what is transpiring in the demonic world, we must understand that many choices the unbeliever makes are influenced by the Evil One. And because the unsaved does not have "light" of the Spirit of God, they cannot always see the full meaning or consequences of their choices. (Perhaps this is one of the reasons that God insists that he judge the outsider rather than we.) Even Christians, with the Holy Spirit available and the Word of God to guide us, make tragic mistakes about what is truth.

I first met Olivia at a seminary where she was helping Christians find deliverance from Satan's oppressions. She had been schooled in satanism from an early age and had been asked to participate with Antoine Le Vay at the Church of Satan. As with many who have pursued satanism, she had sought power and adventure and status. A Christian friend persistently delivered to her God's message of power, adventure, and status. Little by little Olivia began to believe that Jesus held the greater truth, until she reached a turning point and surrendered to Christ. She gained deliverance and freedom after days of intense prayer with the help of a Christian group skilled in deliverance ministry.

Trapped in Darkness

The non-Christian is in darkness. The following story illustrates what it means to live in darkness.

Jim arrived late at night at his friends' cabin. He was exhausted from hard work and travel and looking forward to relaxing for several days with his wife and friends. In the middle of the night he left the bathroom to return to his bedroom. The unfamiliar cabin was dark. Opening a door he mistakenly thought led to his bedroom, he tumbled headlong down a flight of stairs, and broke bones in his hand and foot. His choice, made without light, produced serious consequences—not because he intentionally chose to do wrong, but because in the darkness he lacked the input necessary for a wise decision.

As you read Jim's story, what did you think about him? Some might feel that he should have known better, that he should have seen potential dangers before he went to bed. Perhaps our childhood memories recall an angry parent reminding us that we have been stupid once again. (I wonder, how many of our outlooks toward non-Christians are influenced by our past rather than by the Holy Spirit?)

What attitude should we have toward those lost in spiritual darkness? Jim's church members rallied to assist him and his family as he returned home, but it would have been even better if someone could have foreseen the problem and warned him about the approaching danger, to show him the way so that he might choose to respond and avoid tumbling down the flight of stairs. Christ said "I am the light of the world" (John 8:12). Those who walk in darkness need the light of the gospel as Peter wrote, "Who called you out of darkness into his wonderful light" (1 Peter 2:9).

The non-Christian is in darkness. We are God's "light" to them.

Enslaved by Sin

Jesus said, "Everyone who sins is a slave to sin" (John 8:34). Every person is born into sin at physical birth. We inherited death, the wrath of God, and the sentence of hell. The gospel is our way out. Jesus entered our prison and unlocked the doors, setting us free. One born physically cannot be born spiritually unless the work of the Spirit and the knowledge of God are present. "How, then, can they call on the one they have not believed in? And how can they believe in the one of whom they have not heard?" (Romans 10:14). Again, we must put ourselves in their place. If we were locked in jail, wouldn't we want someone to bring us that knowledge then offer us a key?

Russell was disturbed that his professor of African American history frequently put down Christians. Russell knew that Christians had many times been on the side opposing equal justice. Even so he felt that the Bible did not support racism and he wanted an opportunity to present an alternative view in his class in order that an inaccurate portrayal of true Christianity not influence even one of the students to dismiss the claims of Christ.

Near the end of the term, Russell remembered that his professor had made the remark, "In this class, we want to consider all points of view." He raised his hand, reminded the professor of his statement, and asked for a class period to present a biblical perspective on racism.

Russell was acting in obedience to God even though he was so nervous he threw up three times before speaking. But he also knew that the Holy Spirit was committed to helping him. After his presentation, the professor rose and said, "Now, let us proceed with your execution." The professor then said, "What would you do if you discovered in heaven that Jesus' skin was black?" Russell responded with a thought previously foreign to him. "Actually Jesus was Semitic and his skin color was probably closer to yours than mine. However, the important thing is not what color Jesus' skin was, but that his blood was red and was shed for you and me."

The Hebrew writer states, "Let us draw near to God with a sincere heart in full assurance of faith, having our hearts sprinkled to cleanse us from a guilty conscience and having our bodies washed with pure water" (Hebrews 10:22). The word *draw* in the Greek is *proserchomai*. It is a present subjective active in the Greek language, meaning that we are to repeatedly draw near. Why? Because our hearts are sprinkled[1] and our bodies are washed.[2] Salvation occurs when we decide to receive/believe Christ. We draw near, as this verse establishes, because the sin we were born into as well as personal sin have been washed away by the blood of Christ.

Paul states the case to the church at Rome:

Therefore, just as through one man sin entered into the world, and death through sin, and so death spread to all men, because all sinned—for until the Law sin was in the world; but sin is not imputed when there is no law. Nevertheless death reigned from Adam until Moses, even over those who had not sinned in the likeness of the offense of Adam, who is a type of Him who was to come.

But the free gift is not like the transgression. For if by the transgression of the one the many died, much more did the grace of God and the gift by the grace of the one Man, Jesus Christ, abound to the many. And the gift is not like that which came through the one who sinned; for on the one hand the judgment arose from one transgression resulting in condemnation, but on the other hand the free gift arose from many transgressions resulting in justification. For if by the transgression of the one, death reigned through the one, much more those who receive the abundance of grace and the gift of righteousness will reign in life through the One, Jesus Christ.

So then as through one transgression there resulted condemnation to all men, even so through one act of righteousness there resulted justification of life to all men. For as through the one man's disobedience the many were made sinners, even so through the obedience of the One the many will be made righteous.

And the Law came in that the transgression might increase; but where sin increased, grace abounded all the more, that, as sin reigned in death, even so grace might reign through righteousness to eternal life through Jesus Christ our Lord (Romans 5:12-21, NASB).

Sin separates the non-Christian from God. The way out is not social, educational, or self-help changes, though we must not take up a blaring charge against these. Hear me! The way out is the gospel.

Lost and Found

Jesus said, "Suppose one of you has a hundred sheep and loses one of them. Does he not leave the ninety-nine in the open country and go after the lost sheep until he finds it? And when he finds it, he joyfully puts it on his shoulders" (Luke 15:4-5). In Luke 15 we have three parables: the lost sheep, the lost coin, and the prodigal son. These illustrations elicit a response of compassion as for a child who has ambled off and forgotten the time and the place from which he wandered. We don't condemn an individual for being lost; we don't try to make their plight worse. We love them and we reach out to them.

Because we were lost ourselves, we are willing to shoulder the burden for the non-Christian as others have done for us, so that they, too, can be found. We go out on a search party, willing to drop everything else to find one caught in a thicket. We search every corner of the house, neglecting our daily routine, and we don't stop until the coin is found. We wait and pray for the lost son to come back, for whom also we gladly prepare a feast.

"The good shepherd lays down his life for the sheep" (John 10:11). If you love me, Jesus said, "feed my sheep" (John 21:15-17).

People who don't know Christ as their personal Savior from sin are individuals for whom Christ died. They are born into and are in bondage to sin. Satan has blinded their eyes. They are in darkness. They are lost. But the Bible says there is something else true about non-Christians.

Many will respond to Christ, if they *hear* the good news.

There are not a lot of people standing out in open fields saying, "I need help," or "If there is a God I want Him." But there are other signals people give—their keen observation of Christians, for example, is a clue that they are looking to see if there is any substance to what we believe. Kathy, a friend of mine who works as a merchandiser delivering goods and setting up displays for stores, encountered an evangelistic opportunity. While she was rearranging merchandise, three young men dressed in black pants, white shirts, and tailored ties came down the aisle. She recognized immediately that they were members of a cult. She engaged them in friendly conversation by asking if she could help, inquiring if they had had a good day, and then commenting on the fact that she wondered if they might be religious. One of the men immediately went into his sales talk, asking her questions and explaining some of his beliefs. Kathy, undaunted by the group dynamic they presented, explained tactfully why she would not choose to become a member with them and what her faith offered that their faith lacked. After they said their goodbyes, Kathy asked the Lord to water the seed she had planted and keep those men protected from the Enemy of their souls.

Kathy had no idea whether one or more of the men had ever questioned if they were on the right path, or yearned for someone to tell them a better way. But it's possible that one or more of these young men is wondering about what she said. How exciting it will be in heaven to see replays of our witnessing experiences and to see how that seed was watered, nurtured, and many times bore fruit!

Karen, a college student, sat on a bus with a sorority sister. Lisa had given no hint that she thought about life and death considerations. She discussed parties, dates, grades, clothes, and entered into typical college talk. Karen chatted with Lisa about the last sorority social, then asked if she could share a small booklet with her. Lisa was polite but declined to pray the prayer to receive Christ given at the end of the booklet and instead changed the subject. Years later the two women ran into one another and Karen learned that the gospel seed had been watered and Lisa had become a Christian and even entered the ministry. A Christ-like witness is a precious gift and often results, down the road, in a changed life.

Hidden Needs

Consciously or subconsciously many non-Christians conceal their questions and searching so that we see only their skepticism or avoidance or disinterest. For many it is too painful to keep asking, seeking, and knocking. Some people tell others they have answers, but in those quiet moments at night they, too, are scared (see Hebrews 2:14-15). They can't seem to tell us about these pervasive fears. Many have shut down. They are stuffing their emotions down deep lest they come to the surface and overwhelm them. The right environment with the right gentle, loving communication can provide the hope they need. When this happens many people can let those emotions out and express their fears.

We need to be wary of any temptation to view non-Christians as our enemies, getting what they deserve. Instead, we need to view them as precious people for whom Christ died who are still in bondage to sin, blinded by Satan, in darkness, lost, and looking for answers. *We would not be Christians if someone hadn't loved us enough to get past our defenses and give us the Good News in a way we could understand and receive it.*

One reason some people believe that non-Christians are evil or anti-God is because it's so much easier to think everyone gets what they deserve. Yet, are we getting what we deserve? For me this "suffering of Christ for the lost" compares to no other suffering. It gives us a glimpse into the grief of God for his creation and the saddened Parent's pursuit to find his lost children and bring them home.

Who is this non-Christian?

He may be someone like a dear friend of mine who was deeply hurt while watching his mother slowly go insane. His desperate prayers seemed unanswered, so he closed off a part of himself and blocked out God.

She may be the woman next door to you who is so afraid to ask life's questions aloud that she drowns her fear in alcohol every time doubts start to surface.

He may be the braggart down the street who can't admit his deepest deficiency to anyone. His self-esteem is so shaken that he would rather blame God, events, or other people than face squarely the truth of his mistakes. He's desperately hoping you will come to him and break through his fear.

She's your mom, your cousin, your co-worker, your child. He's the president of a TV network, hoping he can make sense of his life before he dies. She's an executive fighting for women's rights desperately hoping she will feel respected even if that's the only answer she finds in life. He's the homosexual who comes alive only in sex and is convinced God will have nothing to do with him. It might even be you who have never understood that God loves you dearly and wants you to spend eternity with him regardless of your sin, your confusion, or your lostness. Non-Christians need our compassion, not our anger.

Notes

1. *rhantizo* - perfect passive participle (action is completed in the past with continuing results).

2. *louo* - perfect passive participle (action is completed in the past with continuing results).

Chapter Five

The Gospel in Controversy

Christianity's crisis in evangelism is being fueled by the current controversy over the gospel message. Because we can not agree on what the Bible says, non-Christians are rightly confused about the gospel message.

I first met Ella after a Christian meeting. At the invitation to receive Christ, she had rushed forward to find hope and a new life. She had had five abortions, had panhandled, been addicted to heroin, and been a mental patient. Ella grabbed hold of Jesus like the sinking woman she was.

Weeks later at a Christian drug rehabilitation center, her craving for heroin loomed past her resolve. As she prepared to leave the facility for the streets, her Christian brothers announced, "If you go back to heroin you turn your back on Christ. If you blow this opportunity it will prove you never found him at all!"

For the next ten years Ella continued to struggle with heroin while she talked to God as her Father. Gradually, with the help of a methadone program and the prayers of her friends, Ella finally quit heroin for good.

In recent years there has been a growing confusion concerning what God requires of us to be saved and what is the true "gospel." This controversy raises several questions: Was Ella saved? Did the monkey on her back—heroin— spoil the work of Christ on her behalf? What *do* we communicate to others about assurance of forgiveness and eternal life? Is there a difference between receiving Jesus as Savior or Jesus as Lord? How can we explain the gospel to a desperate world in terms that will produce "new creations" that bear the *fruit* of salvation?

A friend who has walked with God for many years recently read a book contesting the simple sinner's prayer ("Lord, save me, a sinner; I receive the work of Christ for my sins") as ample to secure salvation. She struggled for many months with the question of whether she had done enough, yielded enough, changed enough and borne enough fruit to be considered "saved."

Here We Go Again

This questioning of one's salvation over issues of yielding, surrendering, giving up, and willingness to deny all is not new to the church. People have always tried to add conditions to salvation. However words and concepts such as "lordship" have been innocently introduced, but can present a new twist.

Over the last two thousand years church leaders and influencers have produced writings, doctrinal systems, and

Sunday school literature displaying saving faith as the simple, *"pure* reception" of the Good News of Christ's atonement. *Pure* did not refer to the sinner being pure, an impossible feat. It meant the gospel was not clouded with stipulations. Salvation was simply and completely a gift. Despite the gospel being misshapen, added to, and watered down throughout church history, church reformers maintained that assurance of salvation was a here-and-now certainty. This surety of salvation was based on receiving the "gift" of forgiveness and eternal life.

Martin Luther, recovering from centuries of ritually based additions to the gospel—penance, communion, good deeds—wrote: "Justified by faith alone." Spurgeon, D. L. Moody, Finney, Whitfield, and Wesley all taught simple faith. In fact those times when God's Spirit has moved mightily—the Reformation, the Great Awakening, and the Jesus Movement—grace "by God's merit alone" typified the message and move of the Spirit.

After the Reformation, additions were made to the idea of "pure reception." Some taught that forsaking sin, giving up possessions, full surrender, and having Christ as sovereign Lord of every area of an individual's life are essential in order to secure salvation. Immediate and substantive Christian fruit proved a salvation experience. Those who believed the Bible taught that added requirements were necessary for salvation would be considered proponents of lordship salvation. Those who believe salvation is by grace alone are proponents of Savior salvation. Yet the concepts of Savior and lordship in reference to two diverse camps are misleading.

The Heart of the Controversy

Both camps agree that Christ is Lord. He would have to be Lord in order to be qualified to come to earth and die in our place. He must be Lord to wash away our sins. He demonstrates his lordness by offering us the gift of eternal life. When Jesus challenged the Pharisees by telling the lame man that his sins were forgiven rather than saying "be healed," he was telling them that he was Lord, the one who could extend mercy. In the very act of receiving his gift we are acknowledging Jesus' lordship over life and death. And by our reception we are saying that he is the LORD.

Since this is the case we do not *make* Christ Lord by receiving his gift; rather we are believing he is our sacrifice for our sin, acknowledging that he is Lord of our life, past, present, and future. In short we cannot come to Christ in any other way but by acknowledging him as Savior and Lord. But what does that mean?

Those who teach Savior salvation believe the LORD Jesus Christ is received as Savior. The Saviorhood of Christ is believed to be fully adequate before God to secure our acceptance. Saved utterly, totally, and everlastingly by Christ also implies that Christ reached down and saved the drowning one who was helpless to save himself.

For those who believe in lordship salvation, making Christ Lord means that the individual needs to deny sin, abandon his own will, and give up whatever he holds dear in life in order to secure salvation. He needs to exhibit an observable change in attitude, behavior, speech, and actions in order to prove the salvation transaction valid, albeit if the determination of such changes is subjective.

Melanie was raised a Mormon with plenty of indoctrination and formal participation. At fifteen she met a group of enthusiastic Christians. One day Patricia, a "Jesus Freak" according to Melanie, suggested Melanie repeat a prayer with her.

It wasn't until sometime later that Melanie realized she had prayed what is commonly termed the "sinner's prayer." Melanie did not have a working knowledge of Christianity, and can only vaguely remember what transpired in the conversation before they prayed, but she knew she needed Christianity's God. Melanie believed that if she acknowledged her need and asked, Christ would save her. That's when Melanie's journey with God started.

What drew her to Christ was the teaching of God's unqualified "giving" and "accepting" *through* Christ in contrast to the Mormon belief that acceptance required performance.

Church women and men throughout the ages have testified that they "feared hell,: judgement" and therefore trusted Christ. They understood little else. Grace reached down to them at the precise point they understood sinner and Saviorm And they were saved!

Why the Confusion?

In recent years this gospel controversy has become confusing to the lay person and the evangelizer. Well-known authors have taken strongly differing stances while the thinking person muses, "How can they both be right?"

One Bible teacher wrote that saving faith has no privileges, holds to no sins, no possessions, no self-indulgences, but is "unconditional surrender," a willingness to do anything the Lord demands. In contrast another states: "Every Christian should commit his [her] life to Christ. However, no *unsaved* person is asked to commit his [her] life to Christ."[1]

One author proposes to accept, at least in part, both points of view by declaring that eternal life is indeed a free gift, but it is also costly. We must give all that we are, then

Christ will give us all He is, he writes.

Why, in recent years, have believers questioned more often their own salvation and that of others? Some suggest that the change in culture in recent years has spawned the concern that people are entering the church who do not belong. Their choices, it is suggested, do not attest to saving faith and their quality of life after a so-called Christian conversion fails to meet the church's standards and expectations.

During the last three decades, the choice and appearance of sins became more overt. What had often been secret and private sins in a predominately morally inclined society have become public and widespread—infidelity, homosexuality, alcoholism, drugs, violence, cheating, and lying. Depravity and spiritual rottenness were not only let out of the closet, but howled for acceptance. A leader of an evangelical prison ministry in the nineties comments: "The profile of an average American today is similar to the profile of a prison inmate 25 years ago—poor self-image, the product of an unstable family, including a single parent home or where an abuser was present, and where faith was notably absent." This foundation has produced a generation with inner difficulties and inconsistencies, discipline problems, unworthy goals, and crying needs. Its members also have deeply ingrained confusion about the concepts of responsibility, obedience, authority, commitment, decency, and caring for one's neighbor.

With these cultural changes, both witnessing and follow-up efforts took a turn. It became a less frequent experience to meet and lead a person to Christ in a matter of a few minutes or hours, then to see that person blossom into a disciple of Christ and a respectable Christian citizen in a matter of months or even years. Lifestyle choices, formed and forged in the non-Christian, hampered the predictable redemptive timetable in the new believer.

In response many within the church began to pray. They increased teaching on unconditional love and the provision of God while challenging destructive behavior and emphasizing the work of the Holy Spirit. They opened their hearts wider, allowing God to fashion their minds and spirits with added compassion, understanding, and endurance, spending more effort in evangelism and more time and energy with the new believer.

Other Christians, however, began to teach that the church was in grave peril because supposed "believers" were still sleeping with their girlfriends or boyfriends after implied conversions, or falling back into drugs or unable to follow a church leader. Perhaps we were not teaching salvation properly. Otherwise why all the "growth failure" in supposed converts?

One speaker at a seminar in Amsterdam suggested, "We have made the gospel too easy. People are telling us that they have responded to Christ, but there is still much sin in their life. We need to raise the rope, give more requirements, make the standards higher so that people will understand that they cannot become Christians and continue sinning."

From the back of the room a person replied, "The solution is not to redefine the gospel. We all come to Christ as sinners and remain sinners until we die. We shouldn't raise the rope of the gospel, but increase our follow-up of young Christians."

Was the speaker right—raise the gospel requirement? Was the rejoinder right—spend more time with the new believers? How can we unravel this dilemma? We cannot rely on a superfluous examination of the question, proof texting, comparing isolated verses, or working out of our emotional patterns and foibles, anger and needs. Though the following information is by no means exhaustive, we will look briefly at those elements of salvation which most directly affect the contemporary culture namely: the character of God, the nature of sin, and the work of the atonement.

Note

1. J. Vernon McGee, "Through the Bible" Broadcast.

Chapter Six

What Is the Message?

I recently took my car to have the tires checked. While waiting for my car, I noticed a group of about fifteen young men, ages seventeen to twenty-five, standing across the street. Suddenly I noticed one of the boys beating another, the kind of brutal attack shown in the movies. The victim got away and went into a store. I impulsively followed and asked if he was okay.

"Yes," he said.

"Who are those boys?"

"Just neighbors."

"Who are you?"

"I live around here."

He began moving back toward the scene of the fight where a gang-like group still loitered.

"Where are you going?" I asked, alarmed that he was headed back in that direction, perhaps to his death. There was no response as he continued walking.

"Why are you going back there? Don't you care about yourself?"

"No."

"Well, I care!" I practically shouted, when I could see he was not interested in whether he lived or died. "God cares."

He paused. "God doesn't care about me," he said, looking me in the eye and challenging me to disagree.

"He does. Give me a minute. Don't go back there." By now we were only forty feet from the gang and I was wondering what he'd do.

"How did you get like this?" I found myself asking.

"Oh, it kind of happens over time."

"Okay, give me a minute, please," I pleaded. By now I was grabbing his arm. "You're valuable." For a minute and a half before three police cars showed up I shared a short and woefully inadequate capsule about God and hope.

Then he was gone.

I'm not sure whether the young man heard my message of God's love. What struck me about this encounter was that he desperately needed to hear that he was important and valuable to God and that God loved him. Our world is full of people just like him, people who need to hear the good news of the gospel.

As stated in the last chapter, part of the crisis in evangelism is our confusion about the salvation message: What constitutes "saving faith"? As we continue this discussion about what the Bible says about salvation, we need to look at the character of God and the nature of sin.

Does God Care?

Honest evaluation about the nature and essence of our Creator requires that we ask: What was God's purpose in creation? How eager is God that everyone be saved? If he is eager, to what extent has that been expressed? Does God take into account human behavior, its strengths and shortcomings, its abilities and limitations? How forgiving and encompassing is God's love? What is his overriding goal?

Many people would like to know the answer to these questions. Diane struggled with questions about God while in high school. She was so captured by spiritual perplexities that she went to a pastor at a nearby church and poured out her heart. The pastor explained that there are many things we can't understand about God; we need to try to live as best we can.

So Diane dismissed God as impossible to know and tried to live as a good person. In her first marriage to her high school sweetheart she became hurt and disillusioned. In her second marriage she became cynical. In her third marriage she is still not finding that hole in her heart filled up. Each time she has tried . . . hard. She's not interested in hearing how she must try more; she wants to know how she can be loved, how she can be filled up. And if we're honest, that's what most of us want from God.

Sadly, while she was at a very impressionable age, an authority figure told Diane that God cannot be known. But he can be known.

If we are serious Bible students we cannot possibly miss God's persistent activity for our good:

- His detailed provision at creation (see Genesis 1-2).

- His covering for sin after the fall (see Genesis 3).

- The details in the tabernacle and animal sacrifices by which errant humans could cross the wall of separating sin to reconnect with a righteous God (see Leviticus 9:7).

- The fatherly disciplining and renewing work within the nation of Israel toward believers (see Old Testament; Hebrews 12:6).

- The prophets' messages—warning, pleading, and calling people to turn around (see major and minor prophets).

- The incarnation—God leaving heaven (see John 3:16).

- The humility of the Almighty on the streets of Jerusalem and at the cross (see Philippians 2).

- The power of the Holy Spirit available to individuals to instruct and empower (see Acts 1:8).

- The thousands of promises—for love, wisdom, guidance, power, joy, and countless other gifts (over seven thousand promises in the Bible for believers in Christ to claim).

A Sacrificial Lover

The God who experienced pain over the Fall, whose consummate passion is our restoration, and who paid the highest wages—His Son—to retrieve us, is the persistent and sacrificial lover.

"But he [God] is waiting, for the good reason that he

is not willing that any should perish, and he is giving more time for sinners to repent" (2 Peter 3:9, TLB). The word "repent" simply means "to turn around." When God talks to Christians he tells us to turn around (repent) from certain sins. When God speaks to non-Christians he asks us to turn around (repent) from trusting ourselves or any other thing to trusting Christ for salvation.

"Christ Jesus came into the world to save sinners" (1 Timothy 1:15, KJV).

". . . and the LORD has laid on him [Jesus] the iniquity of us all" (Isaiah 53:6).

"God did not send his Son into the world to condemn it, but to save it" (John 3:17, TLB).

"How often I have wanted to gather your children together even as a hen protects her brood under her wings" (Luke 13:34, TLB).

"God is no respecter of persons" (Acts 10:34, KJV).

". . . for it [the gospel] is the power of God unto salvation to every one that believeth; to the Jew first, and also to the Greek" (Romans 1:16, KJV).

"For God loved the *world* so much that he *gave* his only Son so that anyone who believes in him shall not perish but have eternal life" (John 3:16, TLB, emphasis added).

Jesus hated the sin, but loved the sinner. He used the strongest warnings, the shrewdest dialogue, the most revealing illustrations, and the most attesting miracles to insist that humans see their need and the need's remedy. "For he longs for all to be saved and to understand this truth: That God is on one side and all the people on the other side, and Christ Jesus, himself man, is between them to bring them together, by giving his life for all mankind" (1 Timothy 2:4-6, TLB).

God's nature is such that he longs for us all to be saved and has provided the way.

Nature of Sin

What does the Bible tell us about the nature of sin? How does this apply to our message about what constitutes saving faith and assurance?

"For all have sinned, and come short of the glory of God" (Romans 3:23, KJV).

"For whoever keeps the whole law but fails in one point has become guilty of all of it" (James 2:10, RSV).

"Whatsoever is not of faith is sin" (Romans 14:23, KJV).

The Bible makes it clear that all sin—mental attitude sins, sinful behavior, lust, self-righteousness, pride—separates us from God. God does not have sin scales upon which some sins are excusable and others damning. Overt sins are not more abominable than mental attitude sins; lascivious and lust-based sins do not tower over sins of pride and self-righteousness. The strength of the flesh is no more acceptable than the weakness of the flesh. "All our righteous acts are like filthy rags," wrote Isaiah (Isaiah 64:6).

In contrast, the Pharisees of Jesus' day labeled certain *actions* and *words* as sins. They disregarded or minimized the importance of the inner heart response, so precious to God, the pursuant suitor. Solomon writes in Proverbs:

There are six things that the LORD hates, seven which are an abomination to him: haughty eyes, a lying tongue, and hands that shed innocent blood, a heart that devises wicked plans, feet that make haste to run to evil, a false witness who breathes out lies, and a man who sows discord among brothers (Proverbs 6:16-19, RSV).

The psalmist wrote:

The sacrifice acceptable to God is a broken spirit; a broken [ground down to pebbles] and contrite [pulverized down to powder] heart, O God, thou wilt not despise (Psalm 51:17, RSV).

Today some ask: How can you call yourself a Christian and still divorce your spouse, sleep with another, or drink too much? Certainly sinning is serious business and shouldn't be taken lightly. But the questions conspicuously not being asked are: How can you call yourself a Christian when you have a critical attitude, when you are not witnessing, when you feel superior to another human being, when you have unforgiveness or unbelief, when you do not control your tongue, when you are performing out of the flesh, not out of the Spirit? Why not ask these questions if we're going to ask the other questions? Where do we get these standards by which we judge some saved and some unsaved? Are we labeling others' sins rather than our own?

In one church a woman was told by a male pastor that she was tempting other men by the way she dressed. "This shows that your heart has not been regenerated," he said. Yet the minister had a quick temper, often reducing his wife and children to putty. Which was regenerate or not regenerate?

To assess salvation and saving faith we must understand the nature and essence of sin without reinterpreting Scripture to our own advantage. This is difficult work for any of us. When we include the gamut of sin—including as God does, the all-too-prevalent temper, anger, fear, pride, discouragement, gossip, lying, exaggerating, lust, judging, vanity, surmising, and doubt—we all fall far short of meeting this requirement of forsaking sin.

A Call for Honest Assessment

If we are honest, sin still relentlessly challenges our humanity. And sin still permeates much of what makes up the fragile coalition—the church—as Paul pointed out often to the first-century believers. "But I, brethren, could not address you as spiritual men, but as men of the flesh, as babes in Christ" (1 Corinthians 3:1, RSV). Even a cursory reading of the New Testament epistles shows the "saved ones" still ignorant, carnal, fooled by Satan, displeasing God, and self-centered. Christians still sin. In fact Paul repeatedly addresses the saints in his epistles then proceeds to point out the often gross sins among them. This should be of encouragement to all of us who struggle with sin. Because the fact is, *everybody's salvation is in jeopardy if forsaking of sin is a condition because we are all still sinners.*

When one believes forsaking of sin is a requirement of salvation, honest examination becomes tricky: admitting to sin or to a sin pattern or to recurring sin is tantamount to suspecting that salvation has not occurred. When confronted with sin in her own life, an advocate of "saved only if sin is forsaken" replied, "Well, I'm not sinning exactly." This dear woman was doing the best she could with the doctrine she had been taught, but her ability to be truly up-front about her inner life had been short-circuited by a need to practice denial in order to feel secure in her salvation. Honesty is essential if Christ is going to be the Lord of a Christian's life. As John wrote, "If we confess [admit, honestly face] our sins, he is faithful and just and will forgive us our sins . . ." (1 John 1:9). In insisting on lordship salvation are we erecting a barrier to the lordship of Christ in the Christian's life, due to dishonesty?

Is it a standard for salvation that we be "willing" to give up everything—possessions, favor, fame, respect, security, health, and human love? One writer suggests that a person who is not willing to turn from sin, possessions, false religion, or selfishness will find he cannot turn to Christ in faith. Yet, for the most part, we can't know that we are willing to "give up" something until it is asked of us. If we have not experienced testing in an area it is probably not possible to say with certainty that we are willing.

Peter, for example, was sure he would not deny Christ. In fact on three opportunities he failed miserably, denying Christ right and left. How can a person, at the point of salvation, assess his or her own willingness to give up all for Christ? Like other areas, our willingness is like a dandelion that escapes our hands in the wind. If it is a standard of God's salvation, we would all fail. Most people would have to be a Christian for at least a lifetime in order to meet the requirements and maturity level needed to become a Christian under the lordship salvation system. Only *dishonesty* about how the system truly works and deception about our inadequacy to perform would allow one the luxury of continuing to suppose she has truly met the standards of yielding, forsaking, surrendering, and turning required for lordship salvation.

Sin's Solution

The Jews of the Old Testament looked forward to the cross, illustrated by the yearly sacrifice. We look back at the cross now that the work of atonement is fully *completed.* Both they and we found/find salvation through the finished work of Christ and our faith secures the transaction with God.

The problem of sin and its solution were spelled out descriptively in the New Testament with the aid of the Old

Testament, by means of illustration, parable, metaphor, historical analogies, straight talk, and demonstration.

Following is a summation of some of the doctrines.[1]

Problem	Solution
Sin	**Redemption**
Isaiah 64:6; Jeremiah 17:9; "For all have sinned and fall short of the glory of God" (Romans 3:23).	Psalm 34:22; John 8:31-36; Galatians 3:13; Ephesians 1:7; "For you know that it was not with perishable things such as silver or gold that you were redeemed . . . but with the precious blood of Christ, a lamb without blemish or defect" (1 Peter 1:18-19).
	Atonement
	2 Corinthians 5:14-15,19; 1 Timothy 2:6, 4:10; Titus 2:11; 2 Peter 2:1; 1 John 2:2; By the grace of God he might taste death for everyone" (Hebrews 2:9).
Penalty of Sin	**Expiation**
Romans 5:12; "For the wages of sin is death" (Romans 6:23).	Isaiah 22:1-6; Ephesians 2:15-16; "When you were dead in your sins . . . having canceled the written code . . . he took it away, nailing it to the cross" (Colossians 2:13-14).

Spiritual Death

Genesis 2:17; Ephesians 1:1; "Therefore, just as sin entered the world through one man, and death through sin, an in this way death came to all men, because all sinned" (Romans 5:12).

Regeneration

"You must be born again" (John 3:7).

Relative Righteousness

Romans 9:30-33; "All our righteous acts are like filthy rags" (Isaiah 64:6).

Imputation

Romans 3:22; 1 Corinthians 1:30; Philippians 3:9; "God made him who had no sin to be sin for us, so that in him we might become the righteousness of God" (2 Corinthians 5:21).

Justification

Romans 4:1-5,25, 5:1,9, 8:30; Galatians 2:16, 3:11; "Having been justified by his grace, we might become heirs having the hope of eternal life" (Titus 3:7).

Character of God

Romans 8:8; Isaiah 46:9, 64:6; "God, the blessed and only Ruler, the King of kings and Lord of lords" (1 Timothy 6:15).

Propitiation

Romans 3:22-26; "He is the atoning sacrifice for our sins, and not only for ours but also for the sins of the whole world" (1 John 2:2).

Position in Adam	Position in Christ
"For as in Adam all die, so in Christ all will be made alive" (1 Corinthians 15:22).	1 Corinthians 15:22; Ephesians 1:3-6; "Therefore, if anyone is in Christ, he is a new creation; the old has gone, the new has come! (2 Corinthians 5:17).

The Old Testament verifies the New Testament account.

Problem	Solution
Sinful choice in Eden (see Genesis 3:1-7).	Covering by animal skins provided by God (see Genesis 3:21).
Offering of unacceptable sacrifice (see Genesis 4:1-7).	Animal sacrifice (picture of atonement) by Abel was the only sacrifice accepted by God.
Sins of Israel.	Day of Atonement.

Once a year in Old Testament times, the high priest placed his hands on a spotless lamb or goat, symbolizing the placing of sins on a sinless creature (see Leviticus 3:2). Then the priest killed the animal and sprinkled its blood on the altar. This sacrifice, performed on the Day of Atonement, Yom Kippur, covered the sins of Israel. Similarly the gift of God's pardon can come to all through the atoning work of Christ.

The scapegoat in Leviticus 16:10 *removed* sin far from the people even as the blood of Christ's sacrifice pays the penalty due us.

"Salvation is found in no one else, for there is no other name under heaven . . . by which we must be saved" (Acts 4:12). Hebrews systematically argues the Old Testament and New Testament parallels. The sinless lamb of God bearing the sins of the world makes atoning sacrifice for sinful humanity. The writer of Hebrews argues that the Old Testament atonement demonstrated what ultimately became the "once for all" work of Christ.

Is the Bible Inconsistent?

Is the gospel message consistent or contradictory? Does it teach that only "faith" is the means to God? Or does it teach that "faith" along with co-conditions are necessary for God's plan? For example, when Paul writes, "Work out your salvation," is he writing a different gospel than "For by grace you have been saved through faith"? Or is he addressing the saints so he assumes the message is understood to be for those who have already believed and are saved? When we read that upon receiving Christ we have immediately "passed from death to life" and also read "he that endures to the end will be saved" are we confronted with inconsistency? Or is "he that endures to the end will be saved"—"delivered" in the Greek—written concerning physical provisions at a specific point in time?[2]

Whenever there is apparent inconsistency in Scripture, we must either dispute the message as not reliable (because it indeed contains two contradictory points of view) or we must look deeper to see if we have missed something. To maintain that both opposing points—"He that has the Son has life" and that one must master co-conditions to be saved—are true, is inconsistent. Apparent contradictions and inconsistencies can often be understood by distinguishing verses on discipleship and growth from verses on salvation; separating verses on steps into conversion from verses on steps resulting from conversion; considering the specific audience or issue being addressed; and correcting confusion in translation.

Many errors are cleared up when going back to the Greek text rather than depending on a translation. The Koine Greek was developed by Alexander the Great as a military language and included precise and accurate rendering of almost every thought. For example, in Colossians 1:13 ("transferred from the kingdom of darkness to the kingdom of light,") the word translated *transferred* is *methistemi* in the aorist tense, which means a point of time with results that are perpetuated.

For the gospel to be historically consistent, the message from Genesis to Revelation must state the same conditions for salvation entrance. Does it? What happened when Israel had sinned, testing God to the limit in Numbers 21:4-9? Vipers had entered the camp biting the people and many died. When they cried out to God, Moses was told to make a brass serpent and place it on the pole. Whoever looked on it would be saved from death. Jesus said in the first century, "Just as Moses lifted up the snake in the desert, so the Son of Man must be lifted up, that everyone who believes in him may have eternal life" (John 3:14-15).

The plan of salvation (including the problem of sin which separates and the solution in the redemptive, atoning work of God on our behalf) never varies or changes throughout Scripture, from the covering of lamb's skin in Genesis right up to the book of Revelation. "To him who is thirsty I will give to drink without cost from the spring of the water of life" (Revelation 21:6). "Whoever is thirsty, let him come; and whoever wishes, let him take the free gift of the water of life" (Revelation 22:17).

Can We Know for Sure?

Related to this issue is our theology regarding assurance of salvation. Those who believe that it's possible to lose salvation because of unconfessed sin, argue that such a belief motivates us to live more righteously. But casting doubt on one's salvation, likewise, will not guarantee purity. We may work harder in the flesh, deceiving ourselves, avoiding interpersonal relationships for fear of being truly seen and so we mask our true selves. Pressure to be sinless without the *ability* to succeed by acknowledging our full inadequacy and leaning on the Holy Spirit, or without the *assurance* of success because we do not know we are God's children and he is with us, may result in tangled psychological, emotional, and spiritual lives.

Assurance motivates us. Rather than working *toward* God's acceptance, we work *from* God's acceptance. Our energy is spent on others, rather than feeble attempts to placate God with self effort and secure his acceptance. Though as Paul warned, assurance of salvation can become a license to sin, and we are told not to lean in that direction, it is just as surely a very real need and comfort in our battles with sin. For this reason we can know for sure: *Knowing* we are redeemed (see 1 Peter 1:18); *knowing* we have a Master in heaven (see Colossians 4:1); *knowing* our old self was crucified with Christ (see Romans 6:6). "Whoever hears my word and believes him who sent me *has* eternal life and *will not* be condemned; he *has crossed over* from death to life" (John 5:24, emphasis added). We have the witness of the Word and the witness of the Spirit (see Romans 8:15-16).

When we work *toward* acceptance and assurance we have anxiety, frustration, fear, dishonesty, and lack of peace. When we work *from* acceptance, confidence, love for others, honesty, humanness, peace, joy, and gratefulness are some of the rewards. Paul writes, "Therefore, if anyone is in Christ, he is a new creation; the old has gone, the new has come!" (2 Corinthians 5:17). The word for "has come" is *ginomai*. It is in the perfect indicative and connotes an explicitly definite point in time—a time of acceptance we can be sure about!

When we observe Jesus' relationship with his female and male disciples we see a progressive realization for his followers. Salvation is the first hurdle. The book of John records again and again that many "believed in Him."[3] Children pass this salvation hurdle by simple faith. When I asked a proponent of lordship salvation how one could expect a child to meet the obligations of forsaking sin, surrendering all, being willing to give up all, and making Christ Lord, he responded, "For children the gospel is different." But the gospel isn't different for adults than for children. Jesus said that "unless you turn and become like children, you will never enter the kingdom of heaven" (Matthew 18:3, RSV). The steps to salvation lead us back to simplicity and childlike reception, not to impossible levels of commitment and sacrifice.

Discipleship Follows Salvation

Discipleship comes after salvation. Those who lived closely with Jesus often bungled the job of reliable learner. James and John had serious ego problems (see Mark 10:35-40). Martha seemed to have trouble with priorities (see Luke 10:38-42). Peter was quick tempered and over confident (see Mark 14:31). Yet belief in Christ came first for these individuals. Discipleship under Jesus' tutelage came next. Lordship followed. When we bring people to simple faith, we must welcome them, embrace them, secure them in the faith, then we must challenge them that God has more. The Lord has work to be done in our lives.

E. V. Hill, speaking to evangelists at the North American Conference for Itinerant Evangelists, demonstrated the point. He took out a white handkerchief and covered his hand. When we receive Christ into our lives, he said, we are covered with the righteousness of Christ. And when God looks on us he sees us as white as snow. But underneath that handkerchief the Holy Spirit is removing all the ugliness from our lives. And every so often He throws some ugliness out as we are on our way to becoming more like Christ.

One person wrote that the promise of eternal life without surrender to divine authority feeds the wretchedness of the human heart. Actually, divine unconditional love, as a humanly healthy mother gives to a child, releases the human heart from the fear of condemnation or abandonment so that a person can acknowledge God as the wonderful Father he is.

I suspect that if a person says they have forsaken all sin and made Christ Lord of all, they may actually know little of the all-encompassing, inclusive, and accepting love of the Lord. In fact a paradox unfolds: believing they must meet certain standards of behavior, they convince themselves of their acceptability, but they cannot know the all-forgiving unconditional love of the Lord. If confessing Christ as Lord of all (our tempers, inconsistencies, procrastinations, self-centeredness, mental attitudes, schedules, personal action) is required to be saved, then the person who has accurately looked at himself or herself knows they cannot be saved. In fact, if it is required that Christ be the Lord of all (in our lives) then *no one is saved.*

Yet the teaching of lordship salvation continues. Why? Perhaps some whose background has provided them with proper discipline and sociability do not have certain struggles. They may more easily convince themselves of their own acceptability. They have met requirements others lack. This may include their ideas of pre-salvation requirements and assure them of enough "fruit" to pass God's test. Others who desire with all their hearts to live godly lives may be face-to-face with an untamed nature, poor social traits, and self-doubt. They cannot so easily convince themselves of passing over the salvation gulf. David prayed, "Search me, O God, and know my heart" (Psalm 139:23).

Many who teach lordship salvation today came to Christ by simple faith. Years later, realizing the importance of the lordship of Christ, they incorporated commitment, surrender, forsaking, and making Christ Lord as part of the initial prayer for salvation. In other words they have come to Christ one way, "simple faith" and perhaps out of genuine concern "front loaded" the gospel for others.

"Jesus came to save the *lost*," not "Jesus came to save the *committed*." *Lost* people need to be *found*. Once they are found we can point them in a new direction. When talking with a non-Christian I might say that to know Christ is the beginning of a whole new adventure. I try to spend some time teaching new Christians the basics of the Christian life and urging them to become part of a Bible study and a Bible-believing church. But I refuse to fall for the line, "Don't lead someone to Christ if you can't follow them up." In the last several years I have discipled three new believers who moved into my neighborhood within a few years of becoming Christians. Someone else led them to Christ. God placed them next to me to nurture and build. What God helps bring to birth he can help rear. But if it is within my power I try to provide direction for those I lead to Christ.

Is the Gospel of Faith Alone Workable?

For a system to be effective, it must be workable.

If one believes that they will be saved if they make Christ Lord of all, surrender all, forsake all sin, and give up everything, the system gets bogged down with unworkable ideas. We might try to live up to this idea, but how can we guarantee we have done enough to measure up? If we aim to give all of ourselves to God and forsake all known sin, how would we know that the degree to which this was done was enough to satisfy God? How would we be sure we met requirements which are subjective in nature?

Why does the gospel "saved by grace through faith alone" work? It works because it is within the realm of workable. Note the Old and New Testament metaphors for the state of our limitations and inability to contribute to our own salvation:

1. Sheep (unable to care for ourselves)—Isaiah 53:6; John 10.

2. Filthy rags (a picture of our flesh)—Isaiah 64:6.

3. Fallen—Genesis 3:8-19.

4. Blind—2 Corinthians 4:4.

5. Dead—Ephesians 2:1.

6. Slaves—John 8:34.

7. Under Satan's Rule—Ephesians 2:2.

Imagine sheep, filthy rags, fallen and blind people, dead corpses, slaves, and people living in Satan's domain trying to come up with a workable plan to save themselves. Since a sheep can't even find good pasture for itself; since a filthy rag cannot clean itself; since fallen people cannot rid themselves of their sin nature; since a blind person cannot know where he is headed nor how to turn around; since dead people cannot bring themselves back to life; since slaves have not the means to purchase their own freedom; since those ruled by Satan cannot overcome him by their might, how workable can our contribution to salvation be?

However, the gospel of faith is workable!

1. In contrast to a sheep, Christ is a *shepherd* who can lead us to good pastures: "I am the good shepherd; the good shepherd lays down His life for the sheep" (John 10:11).

2. In contrast to the imperfect, Christ is *perfect* therefore qualified to be a sacrificial lamb: "Who committed no sin, nor was any deceit found in his mouth" (1 Peter 2:22).

3. In contrast to having a sin nature, Christ *has never fallen into sin* therefore he is qualified to be a Savior: "Do not be afraid Mary—for you have found favor with God. And behold you will conceive in your womb, and bear a son, and you shall name Him Jesus" (Luke 1:35). The virgin birth exempted Christ from having a sin nature.

4. In contrast to being blind, Christ *sees all*: "I have come as light into the world, that everyone who believes in me may not remain in darkness" (John 12:46).

5. In contrast to being dead, Christ is *alive*: "I am the resurrection and the life; he who believes in me shall live even if he dies" (John 11:25).

6. In contrast to being a slave to sin, Christ is the *redeemer* who purchased our freedom: "If therefore the Son shall make you free, you will be free indeed" (John 8:36).

7. In contrast to being under Satan's rule, Christ has destroyed the reign of the Devil. Christ is the overcomer: "The Son of God appeared for this purpose, that He might destroy the works of the devil" (1 John 3:8).

When the Bible tells us we are to turn around and trust Christ, we turn from trusting self (or anything or anyone else—except Christ) to save us. Unlike us, Jesus is qualified to save. This is why we call him *Savior*.

Who Can Be Saved?

God is not willing that any should perish. The accessibility of the gospel is the greatest wonder of the world. Salvation is offered to those who believe; it is by faith only. No strings attached.

I'm thankful the gospel was accessible to Ella, who is mentioned in the previous chapter. Her transformation did not take place overnight. Though a few Christians dismissed her as "unsaved" and "unregenerate," others stuck with her, teaching her, praying with her, and encouraging her through her early years as a believer. It took ten years for her to put her heroin addiction behind her for good.

The gospel does not require what it is impossible to give. The examples of Mary Magdalene, the Samaritan woman, Peter, and other biblical writers show us our bankruptcy so that we would enter our relationship with God on honest ground. When we reach that point, God can begin to fashion us into something beautiful.

The faith required is no greater than the least faith we can muster—as a mustard seed, the smallest seed (see Matthew 17:20). "Everyone who calls on the name of the Lord will be saved" (Romans 10:13).

Jesus said, "I am the gate; whoever enters through me

will be saved" (John 10:9). The gate is always open.

Let's say one hundred people enter that gate in the next ten minutes.

One may come hopping on one foot, tired out and wondering if he can make it, but he hops through the gate at last into the arms of the Lord.

Another, his head up and shoulders straight, does a little march through the gate.

One comes with purpose and vision for a lifetime of serving Christ.

Another comes with the bare thought, "Just don't let me burn in hell."

One hears the invitation, and runs for the gate.

Another loiters around outside for years, and finally steps across the line, not entirely sure he made the best decision.

Still another starts for the gate, turns back, changes her mind, starts for the gate again, and repeats this process numerous times before realizing she needs help getting through the gate. "Lord, help me decide for you" she prays. A compassionate, tender hand reaches through the gate and helps her through.

A mother won't go in without her children. She gets them ready and as they pray to receive Christ together they enter the faith gate to eternal life.

Another stands restlessly outside the gate. "He doesn't want me like he wants the others," he bemoans. "Maybe if I stand here he'll notice me." "Come," Jesus cries out to him. "It was for you I died." With awe the fellow passes through the gate.

Still another, hurt by the years, stands at the gate, angry with the Master for the way her life has gone. "I don't want you," she thinks, "but I have no place else to go. So I must go through the gate."

Jesus takes them all, because that's how we come—as needy, blind, hungering, frightened, confused, Satan-dominated, lost human beings. Jesus is the only one who can save us. "Come to Me, all who are weary and heavy-laden, and I will give you rest" (Matthew 11:28, NASB).

Notes

1. R. B. Thieme, *The Barrier*, Beraachah Church, Houston, Texas.

2. Passages that are difficult and must be looked at in the Greek, in context, and in light of other clear Scripture include Matthew 24:13, Hebrews 6:6, James 2, and Philippians 2:12.

3. See John 1:12; 2:11; 3:15-18,36; 6:29,35,40,47; 7:38-39; 9:35-36; 10:42; 11:25-26,45; and 12:44,46.

Chapter Seven

Guidelines for the Christian Communicator

As the student drove up the winding Malibu road, the beauty of the southern California hills and ocean view were far from his mind. He was mentally reviewing Christian apologetics—evidences for the deity of Christ, the Resurrection, and New Testament reliability. He was about to meet a world-renowned psychologist, university professor at the University of California at Los Angeles, and author. This brilliant scholar's textbooks were used internationally. He had expressed interest in a paper the student had written, "A Biblical Therapy for Anxiety," and this junior from Duke University suspected the professor would have lots of questions about Christianity's trustworthiness.

As they sat in the professor's back yard overlooking the Pacific Ocean, the questions were more personal. "I don't have this peace of mind you claim to have," confided the professor, "or this relationship with God." Surprised, the student shared how he had come to Christ and then read through a Christian tract based on John 3:16.

This learned professor was glued to the booklet. He read Revelation 3:20 where Jesus said, "Here I am! I stand at the door [of your life] and knock. If anyone hears my voice and opens the door, I will come in . . ."

"That's powerful," mused the professor. After a few more questions, he bowed his head and invited Jesus Christ to be his Savior.

"I've heard about this," he explained. "I've just never understood how to open the door of my life to Christ." He took some literature to share with his students.

A month later he volunteered over the phone, "Now as I look out over the ocean and see the setting sun, I really believe that I'm part of all this. Before I didn't, but now I do."

The next edition of his abnormal psychology textbook contained a short portion about religion and psycho-therapy and included part of the student's testimony of coming to Christ and the difference it made in his life.

Only a Prayer Apart

This Christian student had grasped an important truth. He understood that the distance between a Christian and a non-Christian is only a prayer. He realized that he had responded to the gospel because someone had presented it to him in a way he could hear. He prayed that with the Holy Spirit's help, he would do the same for this professor. This student, like every believer in Christ, is a Christian communicator.

The Christian communicator needs to realize that Christians are the *same* as non-Christians except that we have been bought out of the slave market of sin. We are delivered from Adam's heritage and our previous destiny—hell—and forgiven our sins so that guilt need no longer reside in our lives, contorting and burdening us. Some of us were sinking with no way out. We had tried everything we knew. Someone prayed for us. One day someone said, "May I talk with you about how you can know God personally? God has made a difference in my life. And he can in yours, too." We're on a new path now because someone cared, not because we zealously sought to follow God all our lives.

Who is the Christian? The *same* as the non-Christian except that our eyes have been opened to the gospel and Satan's power to rule us and keep us from heaven has been thwarted. For some of us drugs had taken their toll. We were rescued after several people approached us and implored us to try Christ.

Who is the Christian? The *same* as the non-Christian except we have been brought out of darkness into light. Some of us knew little about Christianity or Christians. Perhaps we didn't like Christians and felt they were hypocritical or foolish. But when we saw that a Christian loved us, we wanted what she had. Slowly our defenses went down and the truth started to make sense.

Who is the Christian? The *same* as the non-Christian except we were lost, now we're found. Neighbors prayed, shared, helped, and loved for years until we understood our lostness. Now we're found.

Who is the Christian? The *same* as the non-Christian except we heard the Good News and responded. Many of us grew up in a loving Christian home where we heard the gospel at a young age. We did nothing to merit this advantage.

Like non-Christians we, too, struggle; we, too, are living in a very human and sinful world; we, too, battle with sin in our lives and still have much ignorance of God and his ways.

We, too, were formed in the image of God. We experience trauma, loss of jobs, marriage difficulties, sickness, the death of loved ones, hunger, thirst, the need for shelter. Christians and non-Christians have emotional, physical, and social needs. We all have sin natures, ignorance, and human needs for love, significance, meaning, purpose, and hope.

We are like the non-Christian, except we have been given an undeserved, unearned gift of eternal life, peace, forgiveness, power for living, guidance, the fruit of the Spirit, the abundance of living, and a Friend. What a Friend!

Before we were enemies of God. Now we are his friends, even his children. The gospel of Jesus Christ has made all the difference reuniting us with God, our Father.

With the exhilarating and satisfying gift of life in Christ we have the *privilege* and *responsibility* to tell others of Christ's offer of forgiveness. Throughout Scripture the goal of believers is to take God's message to somebody else. Paul wrote that the Christian is an ambassador (see 2 Corinthians 5:20) and an intercessor before God (see 1 Timothy 2:1). He wrote that Christian women and men have the authority of the Word of God (see Hebrews 4:12) and the power of the Holy Spirit (see Acts 1:8). Jesus tells us that we are to "Go into all the world and preach the good news to all creation" (Mark 16:15; also see Matthew 28:18-20). He relays that we are people who have power to cast out demons, heal the sick, and take authority in his name over evil. As Christians we are given enough guidelines to carry out the commission effectively.

Paul's Principles of Christian Communication

In order to effectively take the gospel message to others, we must know who we are and what our responsibilities are. This is vital for the Christian communicator.

While studying rhetoric at the University of California at Berkeley, I analyzed the communication of the apostle Paul. In my mind, Paul is one of the most effective Christian communicators that has ever lived, and I wanted to see if I could gain insights from studying what he did. The evangelism methods of Paul are not condensed into a set of rules or a rhetorical handbook, nor are they located in one place. They are interspersed throughout his letters to the churches and in Luke's historical account in the book of Acts. I found his example immensely insightful and identified several principles that have since helped my own communication to the non-Christian.

1. Know who we are and how we can influence the culture in which we live. Paul understood human nature and how to communicate successfully, as evidenced by the results—both the reception and the rejection of the gospel. He resisted using communication as deception.

Paul was born a Jew and educated by the best. He was taught by Gamaliel, the renowned rabbinical scholar of his day. Not only was Paul soundly acquainted with Old Testament Scriptures, but he was equipped with knowledge of philosophies, religions, literature, and skilled in languages including Greek, Latin, and Aramaic. The works of Aristotle and Plato, as well as the many rhetoricians of his day, were well known to the Roman world and most likely to Paul. Paul, as a communicator, understood his audience and the time in which he lived.

Before Paul met the "risen Christ" on the road to Damascus, he secured papers for the extermination of a new sect known as the "Way" that was threatening Judaism. Paul describes himself "zealous" in his pursuit. Though no mention is given as to how he secured these papers, we can surmise that his communication skills were already somewhat developed as he successfully brought about the consent of the Sanhedrin (see Acts 7:58; 9:1-22). Later as a believer he understood that the only pivotal difference between himself and the nonbeliever was that he had encountered the risen Christ.

2. We should be credible, logical, and able to relate to the inner person. The only writings we have from Paul are after his conversion. These include his ideas on evangelism. In the context of the Christian faith, Paul's communication is rich in persuasive skills of ethical, logical, and emotional appeal—he knew how to influence a culture that sat under the teachings of Aristotle, Socrates, Plato, and Quintillion. He was credible, able to reason, and capable of touching the emotions of his readers. Yet, unlike other orators of his day, Paul refused to rely on sophisticated tricks of the trade which could be employed to convince one of either side of a question.

3. We need to rely on the Holy Spirit's power to move us and equip us for witnessing and to help us live our lives consistent with our beliefs. Paul wrote that the responsibility of communicating the Christian message does not lie only with the orator but with the Holy Spirit and the Word of God. "My message and my preaching were not with wise and persuasive words, but with a demonstration of the Spirit's power, so that your faith might not rest on men's wisdom, but on God's power" (1 Corinthians 2:4-5).

Many who are old hands at sharing their faith may gloss over this truth, failing to find any new life in it. Yet even seasoned Christians need to allow the Spirit of God to revitalize the power of these thoughts once again.

God reminds us that as evangelizers we must be full of the Holy Spirit, a difficult job when we take it seriously. Living by the power of the Spirit *is* the Christian life; it is not an added dimension on our good days. Jesus said to his followers some years before Paul was on the scene, "But you will receive power when the Holy Spirit comes on you; and you will be my witnesses" (Acts 1:8).

A woman wrote to me recently that she was afraid of sharing her faith with someone because she might be accused of not being a good example of what she believed. She was expressing a need for supernatural living that would back up her message. She understood that non-Christians would observe how she handled trials, disappointments, death, and fear. These are the practical matters of the dynamic life change brought about by our reliance on the Holy Spirit.

As Christians relying on the Spirit, we don't have to be perfect; but we do need to be honest about our struggles. If they know we are Christians, people watch us keenly. They ask: Are you real? Do you have struggles as I have? Do I have to be perfect to become a Christian? When we are living by the Spirit we can answer: Yes, this is a real life I'm living with its tribulations. Yes, I struggle with it. Yes, God is here in the midst of it—and no, you don't have to be perfect to come to God, just honest.

4. The message we give must be based on the Word of God. Paul reminds us: "All Scripture is God-breathed and is useful for teaching, rebuking, correcting and training in righteousness" (2 Timothy. 3:16). The writer of Hebrews and an Old Testament prophet, Isaiah, agreed with Paul on this assumption.

For the word of God is living and active. Sharper than any double-edged sword, it penetrates even to dividing soul and spirit, joints and marrow; it judges the thoughts and attitudes of the heart (Hebrews 4:12).

My word . . . will not return to me empty, but will accomplish what I desire and achieve the purpose for which I sent it (Isaiah 55:11).

God's Word has power.

As was his custom, Paul went into the synagogue, and on three Sabbath days he reasoned with them from the Scriptures, explaining and proving that the Christ had to suffer and rise from the dead. "This Jesus I am proclaiming to you is the Christ," he said. Some of the Jews were persuaded and joined Paul and Silas, as did a large number of God-fearing Greeks and not a few prominent women (Acts 17:2-4).

God empowers his message despite Satan's efforts to stir up non-Christians against Christians, just as he has stirred up Christians against non-Christians and Christians against Christians. God's supernatural truth has power to correct us and our opponents and reestablish love. It may also bring persecution. Let's just make sure *we* are not the catalyst for the persecution because we have twisted or changed his Word and have offended someone unnecessarily. We are to keep God's Word in God's context. When we do, it has power to change lives. If you have trouble believing this, I suggest you re-read the Bible to gain a perspective and to sense its strength to transform lives once again.

The power of God's Word to convict and the assistance of the Holy Spirit are evident in the following story.

"You'll never make your flight to Miami," said the airline agent in Chicago's O'Hare airport as Rusty stepped off a late flight from California. "The computer has already rescheduled you for a later connection." Rusty glanced at the TV monitor and saw that his flight was boarding. The gate was far away on another concourse, but Rusty didn't want to miss an important church meeting that evening. He decided to run.

Dashing down a steep escalator, weaving among tourists and businesspersons in a long crowded tunnel, up another escalator, down a long concourse . . . he considered giving up. He was tired and sweaty and must have looked silly. Yet, believing in his purpose he hurried on until he came to the boarding area. The jetway door was locked, but an agent decided to let him on. His pre-assigned seat was occupied, so he took a vacant window seat still trying to catch his breath. One minute later a standby passenger sat down beside him and the jet took off.

Joseph, his sixtyish seatmate, was a Cuban-American who spoke mostly Spanish. They began to talk about Cuba. "Cuba needs lots of prayer," Rusty suggested in Spanish. Joseph agreed and they began to discuss the gospel. Rusty wanted to tell him that Jesus was the Lamb of God but didn't know the Spanish word for "lamb." He even tried to imitate a sheep by bleating, "Baahh," but Joseph didn't understand what he was trying to say.

Suddenly the woman seated in front of them stood, turned around, looked Rusty in the eye and said, "Cordero de Dios."

"What?" Rusty asked, puzzled.

"Cordero de Dios—Lamb of God," she replied, then turned and sat down. Joseph, excited, understood the translation. They continued their discussion and Joseph decided to trust Christ as his Savior. Heaven opened. Angels rejoiced.

Joseph received Christ as his Savior because of the power of the Word. The message itself convicted him and it must have had an impact on the Jewish schoolteacher who heard and translated it.

5. We should share our own testimony of transformation. Along with the written Word, Paul witnesses of what he had seen and heard. All of us have the call to speak of our experience with Christ. Note Paul before the crowds in Jerusalem:

> "Brothers and fathers, listen now to my defense." When they heard him speak to them in Aramaic, they became very quiet. Then Paul said: "I am a Jew, born in Tarsus of Cilicia, but brought up in this city. Under Gamaliel I was thoroughly trained in the law of our fathers and was just as zealous for God as any of you are today. I persecuted the followers of this Way to their death, arresting both men and women and throwing them into prison, as also the high priest and all the Council can testify. I even obtained letters from them to their brothers in Damascus, and went there to bring these people as prisoners to Jerusalem to be punished.

> "About noon as I came near Damascus, suddenly a bright light from heaven flashed around me. I fell to the ground and heard a voice say to me, 'Saul! Saul! Why do you persecute me?'

> " 'Who are you, Lord?' I asked.

> " 'I am Jesus of Nazareth, whom you are persecuting,' he replied. My companions saw the light, but they did not understand the voice of him who was speaking to me.

> " 'What shall I do, Lord?' I asked.

" 'Get up,' the Lord said, 'and go into Damascus. There you will be told all that you have been assigned to do.' My companions led me by the hand into Damascus, because the brilliance of the light had blinded me.

"A man named Ananias came to see me. He was a devout observer of the law and highly respected by all the Jews living there. He stood beside me and said, 'Brother Saul, receive your sight!' And at that very moment I was able to see him.

"Then he said: 'The God of our fathers has chosen you to know his will and to see the Righteous One and to hear words from his mouth. You will be his witness to all men of what you have seen and heard' " (Acts 22:1-15).

Because we have the power of the Holy Spirit, the authority of the Word of God, and the impact of our personal testimony, Paul further writes that we can and should speak urgently at all times (see 2 Timothy 4:2), when it is convenient and when it is not (see 2 Timothy 4:3), and urging everyone (see 2 Corinthians 5:18). When we put others first, we don't think of our own comfort or reputation. We can be led of the Spirit to make our urgent pleas heard in the heart language of those in our paths.

6. *We should initiate conversation and be persuasive.* Note how Paul seized an opportunity to explain the Good News.

When the crowd saw what Paul had done [performed a miracle], they shouted in the Lycanoian language, "The gods have come down to us in human form!" Barnabas they called Zeus, and Paul they called Hermes because he was the chief speaker. The priest of Zeus, whose temple was just outside the city, brought bulls and wreaths to the city gates because he and the crowd wanted to offer sacrifices to them.

But when the apostles Barnabas and Paul heard of this, they tore their clothes and rushed out into the crowd, shouting: "Men, why are you doing this? We too are only men, human like you. We are bringing you good news, telling you to turn from these worth-less things to the living God, who made heaven and earth and sea and everything in them. In the past, he let all nations go their own way. Yet he has not left himself without testimony: He has shown kindness by giving you rain from heaven and crops in their sea-sons; he provides you with plenty of food and fills your hearts with joy (Acts 14:11-17).

Like Paul, we need to take the offensive in presenting the gospel. Sadly, our fear, our lack of understanding of non-Christians, and our lack of preparation to present the gospel in an appealing package block us from being more effective witnesses. We do little to maximize our opportu-nities. Where are the books written to the non-Christian in their lingo with their interests in mind? Why aren't we speaking more at secular clubs, political rallies, and in classrooms? It's not sufficient to say, "They don't want us." A more accurate answer may be that we haven't thought enough to effectively relate the gospel to them. Nor have we practiced intercession and spiritual warfare in order to get an effective hearing.

Recently I spoke to eighteen hundred high school stu-dents at a secular Rotary retreat. I presented why God had made a difference in my life and urged them to read the Bible. I was asked to speak because a Christian Rotary member had deliberately asked the chair of the speakers' committee to have me as a speaker. He saw an opportunity for the gospel to be presented, he prayed about it, and went on the offensive. More of us need to do the same.

Many Christians assume that non-Christians aren't interested in our message. My experience tells me that's not always true. Jack Blue, columnist for the *San Bernardino Sun*, interviewed me for a book I teamwrote. It was an evangelistic book, written as a gospel appetizer. In his article he writes,

> The book is better than I expected. I might explain I'm a literary pessimist and am always surprised to find the half-empty book is also half-full. We don't fool around here at *The Sun*. I speed-read it chapter by chapter. . . . I close the book with a beam of approval. The young authors have me sold. I guess I backslid too early.

Over the years I have received hundreds of letters from readers of my books. They wanted to thank me for telling them answers to life and let me know they had prayed to receive Christ. They asked me to send them information to help them grow as a Christian.

The author of *The Other Side of Life*, an evangelistic book dealing with death and hope, received the following letter:

> I am a trained scientist—Ph.D. in chemistry from Ohio State in 1932. I am now retired and living alone (with three dogs) on a hill in Missouri. As a scientist my whole life has been seeking truth and this by proof. Your book started this way. . . .
>
> In her last year Rosemary [his wife] was seeking to believe and I am certain she succeeded and found "hope of peace in life eternal." Now I am seeking. Your book ended for me with the key word "faith." I am praying each day asking Jesus to forgive me and enter my life. You speak of materials to help me grow

in my faith. Will they help me?

The following are comment cards filled out by university students at the end of talks that gave a biblical perspective on a subject.

From University of South Carolina students after a lecture on "Misconceptions of Christianity":

"Your speech really got me thinking—especially the hard evidence on the New Testament."

"I'd like to know more about how to become a Christian."

From a student at Duke University after hearing a talk called, "Is Atheism a Realistic Option?":

"Having the concept of the Resurrection reinforced in the importance of Christianity was a reawakening for me."

Similar responses have come from students and professors around the world. Not all agree with the Christian speakers, but the talks make them think and they appreciate being treated respectfully.

Sussex University, Brighton, England:

"Your arguments are worth listening to."

University of British Columbia, Canada:

"I don't agree with all you said but I understand how faith relates to your topic."

University of the Western Cape, South Africa:

"Please contact me. I'd like to know more about Jesus Christ."

ABU Zaria, Nigeria:

"I am a Muslim. . . . I am interested in knowing more

about how to invite Christ into my life."

Economic Academy, Poland (from professors):

"This was so refreshing to hear about Jesus Christ. Under the Communists we never could have attended a meeting like this on this campus."

Sofia, Bulgaria:

"Please help me! Please! I prayed so that Jesus can enter my life and I hope this will happen."

Sydney University and the University of Queensland, Australia:

"I'm not a Christian, but I won't dismiss them [Christians] as lightly as before."

National University, Ecuador:

"In the name of all the philosophy students here, I want to thank you for your talk. It has really helped us."

Are many non-Christians interested in finding the Lord? Yes! In my experience in the world's secular university classrooms over the years, on the average 55 to 80 percent of the students who are non-Christians have asked to meet with someone to hear more about Christianity after a classroom lecture/talk.

7. We should trust the message of the gospel to do the job and not change or misrepresent it. Paul told the message clearly—we are sinners loved by God and needing a Savior. He wrote:

We do not try to trick people into believing—we are not interested in fooling anyone. We never try to get anyone to believe that the Bible teaches what it doesn't. All such shameful methods we forego (2 Corinthians 4:2, TLB).

Paul also wrote:

[The Christian communicator] must hold firmly to the trustworthy message as it has been taught, so that he can encourage others by sound doctrine and refute those who oppose it (Titus 1:9).

Since the message itself is sound, we do not have to resort to improper communication. A basic rule for establishing trust in the message is to avoid overstatements, generalizations, exaggerations, personal attack, prejudicial statements, or anything that can be interpreted as a faulty premise or inaccurate portrayal.

When I lecture I start with a point of view the audience agrees with, sticking as closely as possible to the audience's understanding. Then I establish a new position by using words, authorities, references, and points of view with which they agree. Then I work toward my own conclusions, but through the audience's line of reasoning. I use *inductive* reasoning, "the process of reasoning from a part to the whole" (evidence to conclusions), rather than *deductive*, "a form of reasoning that moves from the general to the particular" (whole to part, conclusion first, then evidence supporting it).

Let me show you what I mean with the following talk I've given in university classrooms on the "Biblical View of the Women."

1. Women have had it tough in the following areas: (The audience agrees with my premise.)

   a. Economics

   b. Religion

   c. Education

   d. Marriage

   e. Politics

2. Educated leaders have treated women as inferior. (Audience agrees.)

    a. Socrates: "Woman is halfway between man and animal."

    b. Plato

    c. Aristotle

    d. Demosthenes

3. Jesus treated women well. (A small move; audience has little if any built-in defenses to this statement.)

    a. Testimonies of women

        1) Florence Nightingale

        2) Clara Barton

        3) Harriet Beecher Stowe

        4) Margaret Thatcher

        5) Mother Teresa

    b. Quotes of Jesus' claims

        1) Josephus

        2) Polycarp

        3) Thomas Arnold

    c. Eyewitness accounts

        1) Woman in adultery

        2) Martha and Mary

        3) Woman of Samaria

    d. Resurrection demonstrated to woman first

    e. Women disciples (Luke 8:1-3)

    f. Place of women in early church

4. Jesus' accomplishments for women were unique in history. (Audience gives no resistance; curiosity raised.)

  a. Quote Momsen and Gibbon (Roman Historians)

    1) Time of Antonine Emperors (following spread of gospel to ends of earth) most prosperous in history. One of nine reasons: "the unusually high status of women."

5. What did Christ say that had such an impact on women?

  a. John 3:16

  b. John 10:10

  c. John 14:6

  d. Gospel presented indirectly, not preaching.

    1) The biblical writers (eyewitnesses) wrote that Jesus promised to be with us to help us.

    2) Jesus promised a transforming work on the inside that can affect personal direction.

6. Questions? (The questions I get from university students allow me to make further points.)

Jesus said to do for others the way you would like them to do for you. If I am in bondage I desperately want people to help me get out. Sometimes it takes a heap of evidence to convince me on a point. I try to give that gift to others. So did Paul.

8. Be sure our hearts and motives are right. What motives should Christian communicators have for sharing the gospel? Paul tells us very specifically:

Speak the truth in love (Ephesians 4:15).

Make the most of every opportunity (Colossians 4:5).

Holding on to faith and a good conscience (1 Timothy 1:19).

But we were gentle among you, like a mother caring for her little children. We loved you so much that we were delighted to share with you not only the gospel of God but *our lives as well* (1 Thessalonians 2:8, emphasis added).

Though I am free and belong to no man, I make myself a slave to everyone, to win as many as possible. To the Jews I became like a Jew, to win the Jews. To those under the law I became like one under the law (though I myself am not under the law, so as to win those under the law. To those not having the law I became like one not having the law (though I am not free from God's law but am under Christ's law), so as to win those not having the law. To the weak I became weak, to win the weak. I have become all things to all men so that *by all possible means I might save some* (1 Corinthians 9:19-22, emphasis added).

Paul also refuted those who were confusing the gospel.

Stay there in Ephesus so that you may command certain men not to teach false doctrines (1 Timothy 1:3).

Paul warns that it is serious business to teach with wrong motives such as ambition, jealousy, selfishness, financial gain, self-righteousness, deceit, and pride.

It is true that some preach Christ out of envy and rivalry . . . [they] preach Christ out of selfish ambition, not sincerely, supposing that they can stir up trouble for me while I am in chains (Philippians 1:15,17).

For there are many rebellious people, mere talkers and deceivers, especially those of the circumcision group. They must be silenced, because they are ruining whole households by teaching things they ought not to teach—and that for the sake of dishonest gain (Titus 1:10-11).

You, therefore, have no excuse, you who pass judgment on someone else, for at whatever point you judge the other, you are condemning yourself, because you who pass judgment do the same things (Romans 2:1).

Such teachings [false] come through hypocritical liars, whose consciences have been seared as with a hot iron (1 Timothy 4:2).

He has an unhealthy interest in controversies and quarrels about words that result in envy, strife, malicious talk, evil suspicions and constant friction between men of corrupt mind, who have been robbed of the truth (1 Timothy 6:4-5).

All of us can think of times when we had to double-check our motives. A time that stands out for me was when I moved into a semi-secluded mountain home. I anticipated living in a quiet, peaceful neighborhood—a perfect place to write, think, and pray. Shortly after I arrived, a new neighbor rented the house next door. His intentions were different from mine.

John had traveled with his rock band from Texas in order to make it big in Hollywood. He had brought his girlfriend and four cats with him.

John was a drug user. Mounds of trash piled up on his porch, attracting rats to the neighborhood. Rough-looking and strange-sounding characters came and went. One night gunfire crackled as John—high on marijuana—used a friend for target practice. Luckily, he missed. "I'm an eighteen-year-old in a twenty-eight-year-old's body," he confided. Heavy metal music filled the lovely pine-scented air into the wee hours of the morning. Neighbors called the police more than once because of the violence and noise.

Though John definitely was not the type of fellow I would naturally be attracted to, I attempted to befriend him. I had to check my motives. Was I a good person trying to help a bad person? Or was I a recipient of grace offering it to another?

God enabled me to see John as he saw him. I prayed for him and tried not to be angry or fearful of his lurid lifestyle.

While visiting with John and his girlfriend, Carol, over the back deck, a surprising opportunity presented itself. They mentioned, of all things, a Josh McDowell tape on love, sex, and marriage. "Carol's grandmother gave it to us," he explained. "It's got lots of great principles for people who are married or living together!"

John had, of course, "creatively adapted" the tape's principles to his own live-in situation. (McDowell clearly commends premarital chastity.) But that was not the issue to focus on at that point. A door was opened. John and Carol came for dinner and learned about God's marvelous love for them, of the human dilemma of sin and separation from God, of Christ's sacrifice for our sins, his resurrection, and his offer of an eternal relationship with himself to all who would ask.

Hesitant to pray that evening, John and Carol went home with a promise to return for more. The next night they confided that they had trusted Christ as their Savior. Loaded with Bible tapes and books, John returned to

Texas. Only one contact, about a year later, followed. John was still grateful, struggling a good deal, but on his way.

Because I had made an effort to keep my heart right and my motives pure, John and Carol were able to hear the gospel.

Paul further defines this principle of pure motives when he writes that as we present the gospel our lives should be spiritually healthy, not full of fear, envy, anger, unforgiveness, materialism, petty distraction, critical attitudes, and the like.

Those who have served well gain an excellent standing and great assurance in their faith in Christ Jesus (1 Timothy 3:13). [*Experience* is the best teacher in evangelism. Most of us are afraid to take that first step. A good reputation facilitates evangelism as regular evangelism reminds us to tend to our lives and reputations.]

And the Lord's servant must not quarrel; instead, he must be kind to everyone, able to teach, not resentful. Those who oppose him he must gently instruct, in the hope that God will grant them repentance leading them to a knowledge of the truth (2 Timothy 2:24-25).

Let the word of Christ dwell in you richly as you teach and admonish one another with all wisdom (Colossians 3:16).

Be humble when you are trying to teach those who are mixed up concerning the truth. For if you talk meekly and courteously to them they are more likely, with God's help, to turn away from their wrong ideas and believe what is true (2 Timothy 2:26, TLB).

9. We should help the non-Christian see the power and love of God. People are convinced of God's power when they see a demonstration of his authority over disease and the demonic. Paul very often drew a crowd and obtained a hearing by the miracles he performed in God's power.

Many Christians have come to Christ because they have seen God work on behalf of themselves or someone else. There's nothing like seeing an intervention of God in the form of answered prayer, healing, or spiritual power against evil to untie the imprisoned gospel and release it to the masses. (See Matthew 9:35-38; Acts 14:8-10; 16:26-31.) Demonstrations of goodwill have a similar effect. How can we demonstrate this love of God to non-Christians, especially those whom we have unintentionally alienated, individually and corporately, from the Christian hope? The Christian needs to give serious thought to this question.

Paul wrote with eternity in view when he penned: "Since, then, we know what it is to fear the Lord, we try to persuade men [persons]" (2 Corinthians 5:11). Paul wrote, reminding us also that "Christ's love compels us" (2 Corinthians 5:14) and to "preach the Word of God urgently at all times" (2 Timothy 4:2, TLB).

Such was the case when Paul spoke to the Jewish council (see Acts 28:21-25), to the Jewish leaders (see Acts 23:1-10), and to the crowds.

As the soldiers were about to take Paul into the barracks, he asked the commander, "May I say something to you?"

"Do you speak Greek?" he replied. "Aren't you the Egyptians who started a revolt and led four thousand terrorists out into the desert some time ago?"

Paul answered, "I am a Jew, from Tarsus in Cilicia, a citizen of no ordinary city. Please let me speak to the people" (Acts 21:37-40).

In summary, Paul, who wrote that we should witness, also told us how to witness as Christian communicators. We should:

- Be mindful of who we are and how we can influence the culture in which we live.

- Be credible and logical, and relate to the inner person.

- Ask God to empower us with the Spirit for witness.

- Share our personal testimony of transformation.

- Initiate conversation and be persuasive.

- Trust the message of the gospel to do the job. We should not change or misrepresent it.

- Have pure motives and hearts.

- Help the non-Christian see the power and love of God.

As we attempt to be obedient to God's command to reveal him to others, let's be encouraged by Paul's words:

But the Lord stood at my side and gave me strength, so that through me the message might be fully proclaimed and all the Gentiles might hear it (2 Timothy 4:17).

Chapter Eight

Turning on the Light Switch

A Christian couple sat in the booth next to mine at a restaurant. On the other side of them, but within my eye range, sat a young teenage boy and girl.

The couple began to talk about their church and about society's problems. Without much thought for where they were or who might overhear, they discussed various groups and ideas prevalent in America. Their comments were sprinkled with criticism, especially when they began talking about couples living together before marriage.

"We don't want these kids in our church, influencing our young people," the woman said with conviction.

Without realizing it, this couple had just witnessed to

the teenage couple in the booth next to them. They also witnessed when they discussed their refusal to go to a non-Christian friend's wedding because the minister was "not orthodox"; when they called a woman who was getting an abortion a "murderer"; when they refused, while on a business trip, to mix with co-workers because alcoholic drinks were being served.

Whether we agree with these people's convictions isn't the point. Each Christian must make up his or her own mind before the Lord about how to apply Scripture in areas which aren't cut and dried. But this couple was passing judgment on non-Christians in the presence of people they didn't know, and were giving those people an impression of what it means to be a Christian.

If it's true that many non-Christians view Christians and Christianity in a negative light (see chapter 3), what can we do to ensure that we communicate the gospel effectively? How can we best gain a hearing? Again, let's look at examples and principles from life and Scripture.

Use Deferential Communication

When Paul wrote that "he became *all things* to *all people*," he meant that he was willing to stoop, bend, and change in order to score a point and win a person to Christ. For example, we might say to someone who has a different perspective than we have, "I respect that people are multifaceted and support various ideas at different times in their lives. I value the God-given process of absorbing and assessing information, realizing it is not an easy task for any of us. I encourage individuals to think, pray, and make up their own minds."

When dealing with non-Christians we should almost always defer (where possible and appropriate) to their viewpoints, unless clearly directed otherwise under *the fullness of the Holy Spirit.* There are times when the Lord may use us for warning, rebuke, even calling for judgment, but he rarely uses immature Christians or those who are full of self.

We defer to non-Christians in hopes of finding ways to open their minds and lower their guard. We show them respect and treat them with dignity, careful not to label or lock them into a certain point of view. We affirm them so that they might become more willing to consider our point of view. Keep in mind that in general the higher the level of education and intelligence, the more that person wants to make up his or her own mind. Most people don't want someone else's perspective forced on them. When they feel robbed of the freedom to decide for themselves, all sorts of defensive responses arise.

We can affirm people's rights to make up their own minds, as we tastefully present biblical truth. When we do, the Holy Spirit is often freer to work in minds and hearts to draw skeptics to God. (Remember the Holy Spirit is the master at bringing people to conviction.) I suspect that Paul understood this about human nature and that's why he reasoned with the educated, rather than preached to them.

On the other hand, some people need help in making up their minds. They welcome someone telling them that they need to pray a prayer to respond to Christ. When I worked in Watts, California, I lived with a woman who used to be the cook for Diana Lynn, the movie star. I asked her how she became a Christian. "Well," she replied, "one Sunday at the end of his sermon, Pastor Hill said that anyone who had not responded to Christ had to do so now. So I did."

Insistence is also appropriate at a deathbed. One friend, in the throes of losing her father, knew that unspoken family rules must be broken. So she prayed for her father aloud and talked freely and insistently to him of his need to know Christ.

But in most cases, if we must err, we should do so on the side of deference. Deferential communication to leaders and thinkers, makes sense. We'll make inroads for the gospel by affirming the audience and imploring them rather than by labeling them. Affirmation keeps dialogue open. Labeling and dogmatism (I do not refer here to certainty of conviction) distances and shuts doors.

Here are some guidelines for ensuring deferential communication:

Don't alienate your audience. If we label a group or a perspective strongly in our public presentation or private counseling, we may unnecessarily alienate our listeners. In other words, if we judge or attack an individual's heroes, ideas, those he respects and values, or those who have given him identity, we've indirectly labeled or marked that individual as well. (This depends on how this is done, of course. A point of view can be given expressing concern for the welfare of all.)

When I lecture at a university I often receive a comment card from a Christian student critiquing some minor point I made. I am not trying to ignore the Christian, but I am definitely trying to reach the non-Christian. In a draw, I communicate primarily with the non-Christian audience whom I am called to evangelize. I may, however, invite the Christian for a soda and discussion in order to acknowledge that I heard their concern.

One woman told me, "My father is Catholic, as were his ancestors. It has been very difficult for him to grasp the evangelical zeal of many of our other family members. Each Sunday he joins my mother at her evangelical church after mass. Once during a class, one of the best Sunday school teachers at Mom's big church made a very negative and critical remark about the Catholic church. My dad heard it and refused to return to the class."

Even if the teacher's point stemmed from what she believed to be sound Protestant theology, it was not "deferential communication." Granted, in an evangelical Sunday school class a teacher might expect a high percentage of like-minded believers. But there was one in the class who was seriously offended. The chance for this teacher to interact with this man was lost.

Think broadly in our communication, making it the goal to explain things to the person farthest away, the most antagonistic. When Jesus addressed the masses he fed them, healed them, comforted them, and made the gospel so simple that the most errant and ungodly could cross the line into his fold. His illustrations, stories, and points were personal, relevant, and inclusive. His stories about virgins, searches, precious stones, food, judges, and widows were right for the audience of the day. Although Jesus refused to cast pearls before the religious who had truly hardened their hearts and closed their minds, he still hammered away at them for the sake of their own salvation and the salvation of those they misled. Obviously each generation needs new thought in communication.

When we reach the lowest common denominator (the greatest sinner? the most uninformed?) we can reach nearly everyone else, while also presenting a model for Christians as to how to communicate to neighbors, co-workers, fellow students, estranged family members, and others caught in sin. Sometimes it is difficult to get through even to full-time professional Christian workers the need for sticking with the intended audience. Publicity may go out for weeks about an evangelistic meeting. The speaker may have been well promoted on posters and radio. But when the meeting begins, the local group has introduced the meeting as if he is addressing Christians, with Christian lingo and announcements, followed by a Christian song. We can do better than this . . . we *need* to do better than this!

Have an attitude of one beggar telling another beggar where to find bread. I remember a conversation when I had the choice of telling or not telling a young man my own personal questions about God. I hesitated, thinking that uncertainty might scare him away. Doubt can muddy the waters. Fortunately, I realized that this person could not dialogue about Christianity until he believed the conversation to be firmly honest. I told him about my own search, which placed us on common ground and allowed the conversation to go one step further. Another time I told a woman about some of my sins and faults in order to convince her that her sins were no worse than mine and God's grace was as sufficient for her as it was for me.

I often can draw from my experiences to relate to the people with whom I tell about Christ. The pressure to be something I am not is removed when I am simply telling what has happened to me, what I have learned, what has helped me. I can resist the temptation to be dishonest or speculate and simply say "I don't know" when my knowledge has run out. I am only a heart talking to another heart.

It can be helpful to jot down some of the things Christ has done for us such as: the strength we feel under pressure, the sense of relief when we know our sin is forgiven, the help we have when we are sick, and the myriad of day-by-day differences Christ makes. Many non-Christians aren't aware that these are the daily experience of Christians. As Peter said, "Always be ready to give a defense to everyone who asks you a reason for the hope that is in you, with meekness and fear" (1 Peter 3:15, NKJV). Meekness? Why? Because we must not arrogantly look down on those we witness to but with respect and kindness tell the message. With fear? Because we're dealing with precious lives and where they will spend eternity. (Some translations read "with gentleness and respect.") If we suffer, Peter also says, suffer so that your very opponent may be won for Christ (see 1 Peter 3-4).

Draw Circles, Not Lines

This embracing, enveloping communication I'm recommending is not as difficult as it may sound. It encourages individual examination and responsibility. In America, for example, the message that "America was founded as a God-fearing nation and no one is going to take it away from us" is self-serving and should be stopped. It is better to say, "I am concerned with what will happen to *all* people in this country should this bill pass for the following reasons . . ." To parallel Jesus' saying: "What if we gain a moral nation, but lose the souls of its occupants?" Good, Spirit-led thinking may enable us to gain both.

Exclusivity and inclusivity are two separate concepts worthy of discussion in evangelism. Do we draw lines of separation or do we draw a circle including the ones we're trying to reach? In university classrooms I never say "The Bible says you are a sinner." I say, "The biblical perspective is that all people have erred. Psychologists call it alienation. The Bible calls it sin." I get past their defenses, allowing them to hear what I'm saying.

What does Paul mean when he says, "Though I am free and belong to no man, I make myself a slave to everyone, to win as many as possible" (1 Corinthians 9:19)? For some that means staying up late talking with a needy person; for others, leaving their homes to work in other parts of the country as a missionary; for another, sacrificing hours to minister in jail. But for all of us today, it means thinking harder about how to express this God-given love.

Different People, Different Styles

God created us with individual personalities, temperaments, and backgrounds. Because of this we need to communicate the gospel with a breadth of perspective. We clearly see this when we look at the members of the first-century church and compare their styles of communicating with various audiences.

Note, for example, the different style of communication in Steven's address in Acts 7 as compared with Peter on the day of Pentecost in Acts 2.

Notice the strong language Steven used when he spoke to the religious leaders:

You stiff-necked people, with uncircumcised hearts and ears! You are just like your fathers: You always resist the Holy Spirit! Was there ever a prophet your fathers did not persecute? They even killed those who predicted the coming of the Righteous One. And now you have betrayed and murdered him—you who have received the law that was put into effect through angels but have not obeyed it (Acts 7:51-53).

Steven knew his hypocritical audience had deaf ears. The severity of his words parallels the resistance and self-justification of his audience.

On the other hand, when he was before the Jews, Peter said:

"Repent and be baptized, every one of you, in the name of Jesus Christ for the forgiveness of your sins. And you will receive the gift of the Holy Spirit. The promise is for you and your children and for all who are far off—for all whom the Lord our God will call."

With many other words he warned them; and he pleaded with them, "Save yourselves from this corrupt generation" (Acts 2:38-40).

Peter was speaking to seekers who needed clarification and encouragement to believe.

Not only does Scripture record the different styles of different speakers, a close look also reveals that the same speaker often used a different tone, perspective, and words, depending on the audience. Scripture shows us that Jesus adapted his message to his audience. Let's look at two examples.

Jesus communicating with the masses in Matthew 5:1-12:

Now when he saw the crowds, he went up on a mountainside and sat down. His disciples came to him, and he began to teach them saying:

"Blessed are the poor in spirit, for theirs is the kingdom of heaven. Blessed are those who mourn, for they will be comforted. Blessed are the meek, for they will inherit the earth. Blessed are those who hunger and thirst for righteousness, for they will be filled. Blessed are the merciful, for they will be shown mercy. Blessed are the pure in heart, for they will see God. Blessed are the peacemakers, for they will be called sons of God. Blessed are those who are persecuted because of righteousness, for theirs is the kingdom of heaven.

"Blessed are you when people insult you, persecute you and falsely say all kinds of evil against you because of me. Rejoice and be glad, because great is your reward in heaven, for in the same way they persecuted the prophets who were before you."

Jesus looked upon the weary masses, burdened by religion, oppressed by government and unsure of what God required. He spoke encouragement out of his understanding of victimization, his compassion for the weak, and their desire for uprightness of heart.

When Jesus communicates with publicans and sinners, he sees them as the lost seeking to be found and teaches unconditional love so that guilt does not keep the sinner from God nor fear blind the sinner from acceptance.

Or suppose a woman has ten silver coins and loses one. Does she not light a lamp, sweep the house and search carefully until she finds it? And when she finds it, she calls her friends and neighbors together and says, "Rejoice with me; I have found my lost coin." In the same way, I tell you, there is rejoicing in the presence of the angels of God over one sinner who repents (Luke 15:8-10).)

Different situations call for different focus in communication.[1] It is good to remember that initial conversations call for respect and persuasion. Other forms of communication should be kept on the back burner unless the situation calls for it. (This is not an absolute rule. But it often takes a seasoned and/or biblically schooled person to stretch these rules effectively.)

One Heart Talking to Another

We can't "become all things to all people" if we don't care about people. We need to show empathy for their sufferings and have compassion and grace for their weaknesses. We need to listen to them and genuinely care for them. If we approach people with a humble, sensitive, respectful posture they will be more likely to respond to us. They are unlikely to respond if we are elitist and arrogant in our approach.

Imagine the vast differences between Jewish and Greek cultures, lifestyles, morals and mindsets, yet Paul was willing to adapt his communication of the gospel in a way that each could respond to. "To the Jews I became like a Jew, to win the Jews. To those under the law I became like one under the law" (see 1 Corinthians 9:20-21). This does not mean that we change the gospel. However we do fit the gospel to the understanding of the individual. The next chapter takes a closer look at what this means.

Note

1. Paul's communication varied with government leaders:
   - arguing for the gospel (see Acts 26:1-32);
   - in his epistles (see Romans, 1 and 2 Corinthians, Galatians, Ephesians, Philippians, and Colossians);
   - giving testimony before crowds in Jerusalem (see Acts 22:1-21);
   - performing public miracles in the name of Jesus (see Acts 14:3);
   - with deference before Governor Felix (see Acts 24:10-27);
   - before the philosophers at Areopagus (see Acts 17:16-34);
   - reasoning with the Jews (see Acts 17:2-3).

Chapter Nine

A Touchy Encounter

A friend recently gave me a copy of some communication from the world of computer bulletin board systems (BBS). These electronic networks allow users to send and receive messages as well as "listen in" on the public "conversations" of others. Occasionally the subject is religion and, as you might expect, sometimes sparks fly. In this chapter we'll be looking at some interchanges between non-Christians and Christians.

I've included these conversations to allow you to evaluate for yourself how our tone, word choice, and attitudes affect our effectiveness in evangelism. The conversations have been edited for clarity and length. My comments about what is happening will appear in italics. As you read, note what works and what doesn't work. As we pick up the dialogue, Doug, a Christian, is replying to several questions Tim, a non-Christian, had previously raised.

Tim: Is your brand of Christianity the same as other religions who claim to be Christian such as Latter-Day Saints, Christian Science, David Koresch and the Branch Davidians?

Doug: According to the guidelines of what determines a cult, these are cults, not Christianity.

Tim: But these religions believe in Jesus . . . and that the Word of God is contained in the Holy Bible. It is fairly petty of other Christian sects to single out those that are "anti-Christ" because they claim a different truth through Jesus Christ.

Doug: Not only a different truth but a different Jesus Christ. We are admonished to "try the spirits." Read 1 John 4:1-3.

Tim: I do not follow Mormon, Catholic, or any other Christian doctrine or dogma. However, I do have a rather intimate understanding of a few Christian churches, including the Latter-Day Saints. You can disagree with their beliefs and tenets (just as I disagree with, well, yours for example! heheheh), but to say they do not worship and love Christ as much as you do is false, hostile, and faintly annoying.

Doug: Then what is your final authority on these matters? You follow no doctrine, i.e., the Bible, so what is your comparison? I guess it's your own opinion, which in spiritual matters means zip. I could care less what you agree or disagree with. I care about "what saith the Lord."

Tim: Thank you so much for belittling my thoughts

and beliefs. Perhaps I didn't express myself correctly. I do not personally believe in the Bible as the "final authority." That does not mean I don't have spiritual beliefs and feelings. My choice, for various reasons that you either wouldn't understand or would simply use to further insult me, is to try to be logical and objective.

Yes, it's my own opinion . . . as the result of several years' study and thought. I'm not just pulling straws out of a hat; my opinion is based on at least as much time and reasoning as yours, and perhaps quite a bit more. Your saying "I could care less what you agree or disagree with" pretty much illustrates the fact that we don't have much here to discuss. Since *you* know the "truth," your only apparent aim is to tell me (and others) how incredibly stupid and evil we are for not following the same path you have chosen. Well sir, I was merely trying to add my thoughts and experiences to a conversation that I thought had some leeway for outside input. As I've said in earlier posts (i.e., on the computer bulletin board), this conference is supposed to be for the discussion of *all* religious topics, not just those that pertain to the Christian Religious Right in America. There *are* other religious topics, even though you choose to set them to the "sword of Jesus."

I am sure that to another person of your faith, your rigid disavowal of anything not according to the God of Doug is very admirable. To me it is a frightening example of how religious fundamentalist zealots (whether Christian, Islamic, etc.) can strive to destroy everything that does not strictly meet their requirements for holiness. Many people have mentioned their fear of Islamic Fundamentalists bringing their "jihad" to the United States. I am *much* more afraid of the Christian Fascists right here in our own country destroying the freedoms that this country was founded to protect and preserve.

Fascism takes on many shapes, sizes, colors, and sounds. Religious fascism provides much more to fear than the ideological fascism of the 1930s. Being able to say, "God said so" before the ax is dropped does not make it any less frightening.

Doug's reply continues to clarify his position.

Doug: A Christian is one who is depending on the Lord Jesus Christ *and him alone* for salvation. Some who say they are Christians teach that you must believe in God, be baptized, live a good life, etc. In other words, salvation by works. Ask any cult member if they are sure they're going to heaven and they will say "I don't know." First John 5:13 tells me I *can* know. Those in cults are told that it is the sin of presumption to think anyone can know they're going to heaven. This is a short answer to a long subject. Sorry.

Tim: Doug, you said these cults are not Christian. Please clarify this position for me, if it is not too much to ask. Why are religions that believe in Christ not Christian? In fact . . . what is *your* definition of a "Christian"? You referred to guidelines for a cult. *Whose* guidelines? Again you have piqued my curiosity as to the defining rules you are using for these statements. What are the guidelines that make you define the LDS church as a "cult" organization? Doug, you also differed with my remark that Mormons believe that "the word of God is contained in the Holy Bible." You said "Contained in but not complete. An earmark of a cult." Whoa, you lost me there. Not complete? Earmark? What? The Mormons hold the entire Bible to be scripture and the Word of God. What is your meaning here? Sir, if I were a Branch Davidian *or* a Mormon, I would be highly offended by that remark! Good grief, you can't possibly claim that these two groups are not Christian! Not everyone who reads, studies, and prays over the Bible interprets it in exactly the same way. It would seem by your statements that *your* interpretation is the only *true* version, and therefore all others are "not of divine truth." Well, 'tis your opinion . . . and I suppose you're comfortable with it. I fear a day when this country is run by you and your brethren; free will, choice, thought, expression, and faith will be *terminated.* "America the free" only as long as it follows *your* version of the "truth"? No thanks, bud . . .

Notice that Doug does not absorb the challenging statement, responding coolly and lovingly, but takes Tim's strong statement personally and reacts defensively.

Doug: Well, you didn't give *your* guidelines for what determines a cult, but a fine reference book for this is *Handbook of Today's Religions* written by Josh McDowell, a leading Christian apologist. Mormons need the Book of Mormon, "Another Testament of Jesus Christ." Extra-biblical revelation, classic cult stuff. Branch Davidians and Mormons are both cults. Why would you say that I feel my interpretation is the only true version? I have never implied any such thing. Is this how you handle debates? Look, you brought up the subject. Anyone who has read Mormon material can know in five minutes that their Jesus is not the same as the Jesus of the Bible. You say, "Well, 'tis your opinion." I'm not interested in my opinion. I will document what I say if you're willing to go the distance. *(Note that Doug has just used a boxing* *metaphor.)* Sorry you can't handle my responses. I was looking forward to some interesting conversation.

Have you read the accounts of Jesus preaching to the apostate religious leaders of his day, or the accounts in Acts of the Apostles doing the same? True, some folks got compassion and there were some who got blasted out of their britches. Why do you think they wanted to kill Jesus? Because he was always a loving and compassionate Man? Your statement only tells half the story. The reason you don't like "hellfire and brimstone" is because it steps on your sin (er, I mean toes).

Tim is clearly cut by Doug's sarcasm.

Tim: Sir, I care not for your definition of "sin." We all have our vices and regrets; no person can live a life without them. However, I take strong exception to a person denouncing and deriding someone based on their belief regarding "sin." You are free to follow the path you believe will lead you to paradise . . . but I do not desire to follow you. It is *morally wrong* for you to judge me wicked based on that evidence alone.

Doug later tells Tim:

Doug: American history tells us that most of our freedoms were based on and put into writing by people you probably would consider "fundamentalists," and *thank God for them!!!* I suppose you want your lawmakers to be the crowd we've got now, people who are anti-Christ, anti-Bible, anti-morality, anti-freedom, etc. I believe in freedom, even the freedom for you to use vulgar slang. Go for it.

Tim: Wrong. If I have to, I will post a brief biography on each and every member of the Continental Congress and the Constitutional Convention! Not that it would help. There were atheists, deists,

Catholics, Quakers, free-thinking philosophers, and Church of England stalwarts, just to name a few. They had different religious beliefs and religious backgrounds. But they did manage to hammer a set of basic codes that guarantee *your* basic human freedoms. To preserve these freedoms, men and women have died in battle, fought in courts and defended the home front. The Bible-bangers *are* anti-freedom . . . but of a different sort than you understand.

Doug: Oh, really? Does America have a religious dictatorship? Was this country not founded on the principles of the Bible? The only countries that I see as having a dictatorship are those who rejected the Bible. America is heading in that direction. Russia has dumped the dictatorial leadership of the past decades and they now have prayer in schools and open Bible distribution. America has banned the Bible and prayer. We will reap what we have sowed. The biggest enemy this country has is the Lord Jesus Christ. As a nation we have told him to "hit the road."

Tim is taken aback by the implication that he has misunderstood American history. He responds, making good points.

Tim: As far as the country being founded on the "principles of the Bible," boy oh boy is that a can of worms. I would have to say "partially" in answer. Check your history, sir. All of the "under God" stuff happened *this* century. There are general references to deity in revolution-era documents, but nothing declaring Jesus and the Holy Bible to be the law of the land.

Doug: You can read the Koran, the Torah, the works of Confucius, etc., in American schools but you cannot read the Bible.

Tim: Depends on where you are. I do agree with you here, Doug (another shocker!) . . . it is wrong for any of these works to be *banned* from a school campus. But the Bible is not "banned" in every school in the land . . . and for every school that has banned the Bible, there are plenty that have banned *all* "religiously inflammatory works" . . . and then there are those incredibly enlightened folks who have banned such works as "The Wizard of Oz."

Tell me (just outta curiosity), do you celebrate Christmas with all the traditional trappings? Too bad you're celebrating Saturnalia, complete with a pagan Yule tree. Yuletide itself is a pagan celebration, having nothing to do with Christ. Do you celebrate Easter? Aha! Another pagan celebration of spring, complete with animals giving gifts of life . . . having nothing to do with Christ until Christians *borrowed* the event for their own use. Do you celebrate Halloween? Ohmigawd! If you do (or allow your children to) you are propagating one of the blackest nights of the pagan calendar . . . a night of All Hallow's Eve . . . ghosts, witches, and demons of all manifestations are allowed to roam this night in search of pleasure . . . my goodness, how shocking.

Now, you may *not* celebrate *any* of these; not claiming you do. Just making mention of the *lies* that Christians tell themselves year after year, without regard to proven historical evidence to the true nature of many holidays. You can, of course, completely disregard this and claim that my data is flawed but you'll be refuting proven evidence on the history of modern traditions . . . ignoring this proof to meet your world view.

As the dialogue continues Doug does compliment Tim on his willingness to investigate some of these matters. Then the subject of morality comes up.

Doug: What is your final authority on the matter of morality? Your own opinion? Once again, I am not judging you. The Word of God does that (not only you, but me as well).

Tim: Yes sir. I understand your line of thought. But I am trying to explain that it is *wrong* for you to expect *me* to follow your god's word when I do not follow, pray to, or believe in your god and his word. It is *wrong* for you to force me into your paradigm of life and thought. I realize that in your heart and mind this word of god is *the* word of god, and therefore all others are rubbish. However this country was not founded to foster the "word of god." I again beseech you to actually read and study this nation's founding documents (which you have earlier claimed were designed to found a Christian state). This country was founded so that no one would *have* to pray to any given god or method of philosophy. Many of the first settlers were trying to escape the grip of both the Church of England and the RC church. I know you're no fan of either . . . but why should *your* way take precedence? I ask this of you as an American citizen . . . please, for a moment, try to realize that although you have discovered the way that you believe to be "truth," it is *wrong* for you to expect or enforce others to follow that same path.

This is what I am trying to express. I am not saying that you *are* wrong in your Christian beliefs. I'm not saying that your theology or gospel are at fault. I am merely saying that it is *wrong* for you to expect me, and anyone else, to fit your paradigm of existence . . .

and to do so creates a silent form of fascism that slowly becomes less silent, and more frightening.

Please, Doug, do you understand my meaning here? Or will you now say that because I am a sinner my strong belief in freedom from religious oligarchy has no merit?

Tim appears to genuinely desire that Doug understand what he's saying. Doug, perhaps with good motives, has been "defending the faith." But his confrontational manner has erected some barriers that are hard to penetrate. Doug is sometimes saying true things, but too often he is saying them in ways that offend and arouse anger. I maintain that Doug could effectively communicate many of the same truths to Tim if he displayed more love and used deferential rather than confrontive communication.

A Different Approach

During the same time that Doug and Tim were battling it out on the computer network, Nancy, another Christian, entered into computer dialogue with Tim. As you read their conversation, try to note differences between her approach to Tim and Doug's approach.

Nancy has asked Tim his view of authenticating ancient documents. Tim responds that he has trouble with Christians' view of the Bible's authenticity. Nancy replies with comments on fulfilled biblical prophecy and proof of authenticity. She then replies to Tim's skepticism:

Nancy: Just thought the matter was interesting . . . startling . . . regardless of what you think of the "book."

To prove a religious book's authenticity by the scientific method *you* would have to try living by it for a time and see what the results are in *your* life. To try living by it, you would have to understand the methods of translation and application. Doubt that you want to put that much energy into it. But . . . just in case, you might find *How to Read the Bible for All It's Worth* (a guide to understanding the Bible by Gordon Fee and Douglas Stuart) informative. Now don't rule it out just because they're Christians. If you really reject something, you ought to really understand it first. My guess is that you rejected what you hear of Christianity because of all the legalistic nonsense and the "shaming" that sometimes goes with it. Is this why you're feeling so angry? Am I close? (By the way, it's fun to argue again . . . I've missed it.)

Tim answers Nancy's question about why he rejected Christianity.

Tim: As I got further along in life's experiences, I realized that neither the God of Abraham nor the gospel of Christ fit my feelings about life, the universe, and everything. Part of this involved my study of history and the translations . . . and yes, I suppose the "shaming" that goes on with diehard thumpers bothers me. Christ showed compassion to harlots and lepers . . . show me the "Christian" who does the same in this modern age. They *do* exist and I've had the honor of knowing a few. But they are *not* those who roam around speaking hellfire and brimstone.

Note that Tim feels comfortable enough with Nancy to share his feelings.

Nancy: Care to share your world view . . . life, the universe, and everything, e.g., how do you identify *your* purpose and meaning? My adult daughter thinks mine is to be a "mom." I tend to mother birds, dogs, and in the past some unusual people with interesting needs. I guess I see mine as "being" me at least as much of the time as I can be honest and transparent. The doing kind of comes out of that.

Tim shares some of his thoughts and then expands on his skepticism regarding the Bible.

Tim: I don't dismiss anything simply because "the originals" are gone. We were chatting about this topic a while back and that's what I was referencing. There are many valuable records of the past, some that have gone through translations, some that have been passed down verbally, etc.

However, with any *real* study of the Bible (the particular document that Doug and I have been chatting about) a sane, rational thinking person will realize that the modern Bible *is not the literal word of God*.

There, Doug, did I [vulgarity] ya off enough? I really don't mean to . . . just stating fact (as you claim to).

Anyway, Nancy, with this particular subtopic I am not debating the worth, value, or merit of the Bible . . . just the assertion that this book, as it sits before me (got a copy of the KJ right here for what it's worth) is *not* the *literal* word of the Creator. As we've discussed more in the past, I take further exception to the content, based on political and social slants of the time, and have simply been trying to talk about it as a work of man, which it is. As a work of man, it must be realized that everything contained within is colored, or tainted, with the emotions, thoughts, laws, and events of the period in which it was created. Since then it has been tainted and bastardized by the various translations, interpretations, etc., that it has undergone.

Oh well . . . I'm sure to get a nasty response from Doug . . . or maybe he just feels that I am such an idiot I don't even warrant a response. His privilege to think so, I suppose! hehehehe.

Again, as we've chatted about in the past, my *main* reason for even giving a care about this topic is my fear of fundamentalist Christians using their "law" to influence the laws of this nation. People who are so convinced of what God wants for his creation become convinced that it is *their* job to force the rest of mankind into "God's Plan." However they often do it through very subtle means . . . and the majority of people in this country take their freedoms for granted. If they would open their eyes, they would notice that in only the last one hundred years American citizens' rights have slowly been ripped away, right in front of their noses.

Fundamentalist, Bible-thumping, Koran-waving (or whatever faith/book they use) religious Zealots are trying very hard to bring this country down. The sad thing is the damage that is being done from within.

Oh well . . . enough about this for now.

P.S. Drive a conservative crazy: Ask him to think for himself!

Nancy: Couldn't agree more . . . but then it's a real maturity issue. Being a carrier of God's grace is supposed to be the first in a series of stages a Christian believer goes through, but I don't think it hit me until I was in my forties. Jesus must be going to come back, if he lives (which I believe he does). He's got to be as fed up with the mess as you and I are. Am currently studying "spiritual passages" . . . interesting stuff.

Actually, Jesus is the Word of God.

I think you're waaaaay too negative about the Bible.

Even if you don't buy the "inspired" idea, there are men and women who lived, who loved, who tried to follow a God they had encountered and failed periodically—not so different from you or me. I think there's a lot of wisdom there for living life as a human being. It helps if Jesus is the grid that interprets the rest.

Tim: Ah . . . but you see, my point (as it pertains to this thread) is not about the meaning of the Bible, its teachings, tenets, and advice. Nope. My comments were directed at Doug because he *does* hold it to be the literal law and word of God.

Sorry, Nancy . . . wasn't trying to be generally "Bible-negative." I was taking exception to Doug's concept of ultimate truth . . . because it is a beautiful example of the type of blind zealotry that can create religious dictatorships.

Notice how Tim softens his stance when he knows he's being heard. Nancy tries a more personal approach with Tim, but Tim is not ready.

Nancy: How would your life change if you accepted Jesus as a grid for interpreting the Bible?

Tim: Fairly dramatically, I suppose. Sorry . . . not interested. Thanks for trying, though . . . Well, there's another sin I'll have to fax to my priest.

Nancy: The pleasure was mine. Thanks for giving it some thought.

Nancy has developed a rapport with Tim that allows her to disagree with him tactfully. She has deferred to him enough that he senses she affords him human dignity and respect. As a result, even in spite of his resistance to the gospel, she can gently ask him about his own salvation. He politely declines to pursue the personal issue but thanks her for trying. Nancy has deferred to

Tim, communicated truth in love, and left the door open for the Holy Spirit to work. Perhaps the next sensitive Christian he encounters will help nudge him even closer to the kingdom.

Not long after Doug and Nancy each conversed with Tim, Nancy and Doug got into a computer conversation with each other about how Christians should communicate truth. As we pick up the dialogue, we see that Nancy has tried gently to suggest to Doug his need for more sensitivity and tact.

Nancy: Doug, concerning using the Scriptures when dealing with people, if one is sensitive to the Holy Spirit and dealing with the "truth" in "love," then I agree with you completely. If, however, one simply knows some Scripture to quote for certain circumstances and does so to prove a point or with an "us/them" mentality, I have significant doubts as to what can be expected as results. I believe God is displeased with a Christian pattern of putting those who have accepted Christ as Savior in a superior position to those who have not. All of us are created in the image of God and are searching for meaning and purpose. If we can give our neighbor a helping hand in that search, that's one thing, but if we exalt ourselves in some egotistical way, we hinder the gospel. To the religious bigots of Christ's time, he hammered on them pretty hard. But to those who were searching/seeking or were victims, he (meek and lowly of heart) came as one of them.

Doug compliments her.

Doug: An excellent response! And I agree with you. I am going to stick my neck out and assume you think I am the one who is being "egotistical" and "superior." If you are, I disagree. The key is as you said, those who are "seeking meaning and purpose." Sometimes it's difficult to tell, but I've dealt with lots of people in (BBS) religion conferences and after a while you can tell who is sincere and who is not. When a person belittles Jesus Christ, the Bible, and other doctrines by being sarcastic, rude, vulgar, etc., then I doubt they're "searching." I deal with these types in a harder way. I believe this is Scriptural. If a person is sincere, I can be as gentle as a lamb. Most people who are in religion conferences are there for who knows why, but generally it is to belittle those who have Jesus Christ and the Bible as their higher authority.

Nancy had also commented about shame.

Nancy: "Shame" is an interesting phenomenon. When shame is "healthy," it tells us where our personal boundaries are and where others' boundaries are so we don't offend or abuse one another. When shame is "unhealthy," we feel defective without any remedy. Both Christians and non-Christians suffer from unhealthy shame. The Bible calls it condemnation. Guilt has more to do with moral behavior—the moral absolutes we violate. Therefore, when a person tries to share the gospel in America, they have to be willing to become a friend, an equal, if they want to avoid the "shame barrier" that over 90 percent of us deal with. This involves being "real" . . . "transparent" . . . admitting our own doubts and difficulties as we live the life of faith in Jesus Christ.

Doug again compliments her.

Doug: Good response. I appreciate the time it took to respond. "Healthy" shame is Bible shame. Conviction of sin brings shame, as it should. As to becoming a friend, yes, this sometimes applies, but also sometimes you have to rise above personalities to proclaim the whole counsel of God. In preaching, this involves exhortation, rebuking, etc. Church discipline is to be given so that shame and yes, guilt, is to be felt by the offender. This is to bring him to repentance and back into fellowship with the local church.

Nancy summarizes her reactions to Doug's statements.

Nancy: My assumption was that you were egotistical. I based this on what appeared to be an unwillingness to draw out the other person to see if there were some things you could affirm. It appeared that you simply reacted to what they said and with arguments that were non-relevant from their perspective.

Recall that Doug had felt that many participate in computer BBS religion conferences to belittle Christians and the Bible. Nancy comments.

Nancy: Perhaps, but I also think they are interested in why Christians believe what they do and why they think the way they do. Whether a person is seen as belittling Christians or not, they are created in the image of God and deserve respect, i.e., at least listening and asking them to expand on their beliefs.

Then Nancy responds to Doug's assertion that "Conviction of sin brings shame, as it should."

Nancy: Here we part ways. Conviction of sin brings guilt which is remedied by the finished work of Jesus Christ. Unhealthy shame is a product of human experience, such as parents telling us "we'll never amount to anything." As children, we internalize such pronouncements and even as believing Christians we can feel hopeless about remedy. Here grace is the remedy—knowing that we are loved and accepted by God because of who we are. Since Christ died for us "while we were sinners," God's love is to be demonstrated to those who do not accept Christ and even those who belittle us. Since much of our culture is bound in unhealthy shame, to come to one who does not accept Christ from a perspective of perceived superiority is to trigger a shame barrier and an angry reaction in that one which prevents them from seeing/hearing the God we love and serve speaking through us.

If the gospel is to penetrate secular culture, it will have to be because love is demonstrated in a way that goes beyond the human kindness we all offer. There may be a time to be firm, but only after love has played itself out.

Nancy realized something that Doug did not: Often people mask their true feelings to protect themselves or to test others. Nancy understands that the warmth of gentle love often coaxes the most reluctant bud to open and blossom. Of course Christians should be ready to give an account for the hope that is in them. But is Doug finding his personal security in "having the right answer," "standing up for the faith," and "defending the truth" rather than trusting Christ for the security to be selective, sensitive, warm, and loving toward Tim and other skeptics?

Redeeming Compassion

Here is a final example of "love playing itself out." Nancy is now talking via computer with Yemi, a young man who told her that he has had a negative experience with Christians.

Yemi: Nancy, I agree, many people tend to use the "Word of God" to batter and shame others. I have seen it happen to many people and it has happened to me. I went to a school that was full of rich kids and they were all Christian. I was not. They beat me up and told me that would happen until I became a

Christian. I told the principal and he said, "Boys will be boys!" I soon became mentally abused to boot. I went "crazy" and had to go back to my other school. My mother was so mad at me because she had to drive me every day. I was in the sixth grade and my mother started hating me because God told her to, unless I became a Christian. I went born again by seventh grade and by eighth grade I had renounced religion until I could figure what it is all about. Here I am today, the day after Easter Sunday, depressed out of my mind, because my own family won't have me unless I give up my rights and values. I don't have a house. I am staying with a friend, and his mother doesn't like me. But on Easter Sunday I woke up and found an Easter basket sitting next to me where I sleep.

Nancy is shocked.

Nancy: This is the worst abuse I've ever heard of. Are you pulling my leg, or is it really true? I'm speechless. Jesus would put his arms around you and ask your forgiveness for the behavior of these others. He would listen to you for hours and hours and make gentle comments about God, accepting you throughout the encounter. May I be a stand-in for Him and on behalf of these "Christians," "Will you forgive us for our bigoted, fear-bound, immature, and unchristian behavior?" You are a person of infinite value and one to be treasured, not abused. You have suffered the same torture Jesus did by the "religious" community. You're welcome at our house anytime (except after bedtime, of course). There's plenty of love here.

Yemi is truly touched by Nancy's compassion toward him.

Yemi: Nancy, you show much more of the compassion that (as I see it) a true Christian has. You are much more accepting than many, and you praise all as if they were personal friends. This is closer to how I would like to be seeing Christians today. I think that most "Christians" give Christianity a bad name. You are much "closer" to God than others I have met and talked with. Although I disagree with you about some things, I like your attitude . . . chat at you later.

Nancy: Thanks for the affirmation . . . must be "affirm Nancy" week . . . I'm getting many good wishes. Don't we all need them? I believe Jesus would be this way and was when he walked the earth. Wish I could communicate him better so others could know, love, and be loved by Him, too.

Who Is God?

Later, Nancy is able to talk with Yemi about God. Note how Nancy tries to communicate within Yemi's frame of reference and vocabulary.

Yemi: Basically it is so true what you said around the lines of "Man was made in the image of God, and we are here to find out the truth as we see it." (Close to that at least.) I have not found my God but you have found yours. It is an individual thing. No one opinion can be wrong about God, but none of them can be totally right either. In my opinion (as I've seen God so far) God is not an actual entity, but an Energy. He exists within everything, but we can't transcend this material plane to actually see him as a whole. We can only perceive little bits of him as we travel through this plane of existence. We "become one with God" when we die, only because our spirit is able to transcend the material desires and lusts of this plane. Some are able to almost do this on this plane, but not quite. God is all, but God is nothing. He is truth and he is lie. He is good and he is evil. God is all but God is nothing. He is only energy, he has no solid form, and we cannot think on the level "required" to under-stand "God."

Nancy: My experience has been somewhat similar. God is all yet transcends the creation as God is Creator. God is truth and exposes the lie. God is Good and is at work conquering evil which is a natural occurrence when free will is an aspect of Creation and the beings can choose selfishly. God releases us from creation's requirement of perfection in order to be at one with God, through our accep-tance of Jesus who was able to be in all ways human yet without distortion of the image of God. That is, Jesus clothes us in perfection so we can experience oneness with God to some extent even in these imperfect bodies and souls. God is Spirit and has no solid form, although God took on the form of Jesus to clarify God's character and ways.

Nancy now responds to Yemi's remarks about God being an Energy and our inability to totally perceive him.

Nancy: On most of this we can see eye to eye: God is everywhere and we, being limited beings, cannot per-ceive the ALL . . . the infinite . . . yet we get glimpses which can be profound. Whether Energy and Spirit are the same, I can't say . . . I'm just ignorant. As I have encountered God in my inner being, I have come to know something of the character of God, i.e., faithful, wise, powerful, creative, without darkness or evil, just, and above all loving. These encounters transcend rational thought but can be reflected on rationally. I can see why someone might call this Energy, it is unseen but it is power.

Next, Nancy speaks to Yemi's assertion that "we become one with God when we die."

Nancy: As I understand from my view, we become one with God gradually in this life as we yield to the Spirit of God and walk more and more congruently with the image of God in which we are all created. Even so, we maintain our distinctions as children of God. Jesus managed to do this and achieved the one-ness in this life. It does involve accepting our desires and lusts, yet being yielded enough to God's Spirit to be free to choose whether to satisfy those desires and lusts or to transcend them for Love's sake . . . love of God and love of self/neighbor.

The help Jesus gives me is that he died and was brought back to life and now lives in the spiritual dimension, sending into our inner being (if we ask) the Spirit of God in a personal way so that we are empowered (energized) to respond to the Spirit and transcend the natural if we yield to the Spirit. (Hope this doesn't sound like a lot of gobble-de-gook.) Funny that one wants to run from this kind of love . . . it requires such a yielding and letting go of being in con-trol which we all need to feel to some degree at least.

* * *

We can draw several conclusions from these inter-changes. Tim's and Yemi's intelligent thinking about spiri-tual things demonstrates that nonbelievers can be sincere in their search for truth. It is simply not true that all non-believers are uninterested in spiritual things. Tim and Yemi sure were! However, the difference in Tim's response to Doug and his response to Nancy reveals how our approach can either antagonize and build walls, thus preventing us from being able to effectively share Christ, or it can affirm and build bridges so that we can give the gospel to a recep-tive audience. Our attitude is key. Nancy was able to side-step certain emotional hooks and kept the right focus. Her communication is a good illustration of what we've been talking about in this book.

Isn't evangelism communicating Christ so others can know, love, and be loved by him, with the result of a life gradually changing to be pleasing to God? Doesn't it make sense to avoid personal defenses, unstudied and unreflective responses, and insensitivity in order that God's love might be seen?

Chapter Ten

Let's Clean House!

A couple of years ago the National Religious Broadcasters Convention in Los Angeles, California, featured "Hollywood Night." While attending the event I learned there are three or four thousand Christians in Hollywood who are involved in Christian groups or churches, trying to reach the non-Christian with the gospel.

The concern that night was not the "immoral film industry," but for those in Hollywood who need Christ. This was a gathering of Christians within the industry who wanted to be the "light" and asked for our prayers.

As I sat and listened, I couldn't help but think about the contrast between how these actors and directors saw and related to the people in Hollywood and how many Christians often talk about reporters and journalists in the secular media. We portray the media as ungodly and anti-Christian, but is that really the case?

One reporter says,

A large segment of good journalists simply turn off moral information. It's as if they are tone deaf in this area. They don't understand Christian doctrine and they don't really understand the Judeo-Christian ethic. Since they don't understand it, they find difficulty in interpreting it fairly.[1]

Evangelical Peggy Wehmeyer, the first religion reporter on ABC-TV, comments,

Many people say to me, "The media are so biased—they don't cover our new church dedication; they just hate Christians." Well that's taking it too far. Christians have to learn how to work *with* the media and to understand how television works. They need to learn why you must have visuals, how to say things in a minute and a half and what is significant to a secular audience. If you can't learn to play this game, you may be left out of the game.[2]

As I recall that "Hollywood Night" and write these words, I wonder: Is there a ministry to reach the secular journalists? Is there a ministry to reach feminists or members of the American Civil Liberties Union or the "liberals"?

Christians urgently need inroads for the gospel into cultural groups, and particularly for the leaders of these groups. Who can contact leaders in the various cults, in the New-Age movement, in MTV and the rock music world, or among TV producers? Who will try to reach the news anchors or the leaders in the feminist National Organization for Women with the Good News? Who will reach these people in *your* nation?

I pray earnestly that the "Lord of the Harvest" will send laborers to evangelize our world's mega-culture. I pray that those who read this book will be impressed with the urgency of the need both to present the gospel with power and have an impact on social and political problems. To that end, let me make several suggestions:

1. Study the non-Christian until you know the people you are led to reach better than they know themselves. Join secular groups, pray for insight, interview non-Christians. (A survey and audience analysis sheet are provided at the end of this book for this purpose.)

2. Next take out a thesaurus and find fresh words to express your faith, keeping in mind hot buttons, prejudices, and needs of your audience. Go to the library and read current books. Find common perspectives from which to reason. Learn new vocabulary to communicate timeless ideas.

3. Keep sharing your faith. The Bible says "He who wins souls is wise" (Proverbs 11:30). Some teach that the Hebrew allows for two renderings of this verse: If you are wise you will win souls; and if you win souls, you'll become wiser in the process.

4. Ask for God's guidance regarding your purpose and priorities. When it comes to the dilemma concerning our call to evangelism and the pressing social issues and needs, there might be four possible directions in which to head. You may be led by God to choose one or a combination.

First: Choose our battles. We may decide not to become involved in public issues for the sake of the gospel. If we make this choice we should not feel guilty that we have opted out of social reform. The *preponderance* of biblical data is on the side of *evangelism* over participation in social issues.

Paul was determined to make his trek to see Caesar. He felt it was advantageous to reason his faith with leaders of the Roman Empire. There were many social issues he could have confronted—from taxation to slavery—but his call was to evangelism. He stuck to his call. The first-century Christians turned the world upside down by preaching not a reform, but a transformation. We must be led of the Spirit on issues, but we must *never neglect evangelism.*

Reread the New Testament and let God speak with you. What battlefield is he calling you to?

Second: We can choose to participate in social issues but not make them an issue in witnessing. If we are involved in controversial issues it doesn't need to come up in witnessing conversations nor does it need to be such a public part of our life that it would obstruct our witness to the people we are trying to reach. In other words we don't start sharing the gospel and end up giving a tirade against homosexuals.

Third: We can learn bridge-building communication. We can articulate why we feel as we do about abortion and other issues in a way that respects other people and loves them. Remember: "Grievous words stir up anger; but a soft answer turns away wrath" (Proverbs 15:1). We can use issues as a path to the gospel, not away from it. Heather, a Christian in Texas, tells of a powerful right-wing Christian activist who, by his manner, turns off nonbelievers, political moderates, and other Christians. People see him as pushy and underhanded and therefore do not accept his gospel.

Conversely a group of women stood outside an abortion clinic. A guard was posted there to protect the clinic and its patrons. Some of the Christians made friends with the guard. They talked with him, brought him cookies and even knitted him a sweater for Christmas. Because of their loving concern the guard came to know Christ. He gave up that job and joined the Christians.

If Christians come across as self-protecting and self-serving, and many think we are, the rest of what we say will not be heard. How do the love of God and our love communicate amidst social topics that we really bring Good News?

Fourth: We can pray. We can ask God to reveal our sins to us and repent, entering into humility from which we can reach the lost. Pray daily, fervently, and passionately for the country we inhabit and go full speed ahead in evangelism.

Search Your Heart

We must forgive and unlock the gridlock in evangelism. I would invite you to take a few minutes or a few hours sometime soon (right now, if possible) to ask the Lord to search your heart concerning anyone, or any group you hold a grudge against. Whom do you need to forgive and release from your anger?

Following is a checklist:

homosexuals/lesbians
liberals
feminists
president/prime minister/premier/etc.
politicians
secular humanists
professors
actors/actresses
secular media
Planned Parenthood
abortionists
American Civil Liberties Union

Parent/Teachers Association
Congress/Senate/Parliament
those living together without marriage
immoral
drug pushers
drunk drivers
New-Agers
Christians who think differently than we do
insensitive Christians
Others: _____

"Love your enemies, do good to those who hate you, bless those who curse you, pray for those who mistreat you" (Luke 6:27-28).

The church is in need of housecleaning in evangelism, to clear out the cobwebs and return to the presentation of the glorious gospel of Jesus Christ. In so doing we must remember that Christianity isn't a club for the elite. It does not have restricted membership. It does not support a snob mentality or wear an "I'm better than you" (nor "I'm worse than you") badge. The club is open to all—that is, everyone who will understand God's offer of forgiveness and eternal life and respond. We are the mail carriers of that letter of hope.

For those who have struggled with evangelism issues, laboring in prayer, searching one's heart, trying to stay in touch with the unbeliever, and represent the love of God, may I say that your victories amidst such confusion are very commendable. And for those who have fought for social issues and families, it is understood that your work has been well-motivated and is appreciated.

As we deliver the gospel message we should remember that many will respond if our prayers and lives are

Spirit-powered and our message is loving, relevant, and convincing. If our listener is offended let's continue to make sure that the true "gospel" is the only offense, not our lives, our judgments, the issues, the viewpoint about country, our sin, our own un-Christlike attitudes, our inadequate communication, our exclusivity, our erroneous views of the non-Christian, our lack of love, our intolerance, our isolation, our selectivity, our morals, our preoccupation with self and family, our hypocrisy, or our sloppy thinking.

Together, let's clean house!

Notes

1. Wes Pippert, quoted in Collen Cook, *All that Matters* (Chicago: Moody Press, 1992), 41.

2. Interview with Peggy Wehmeyer, conducted by David Ness, executive editor, *Christianity Today*, 15 August 1994, 16.

Appendix

Survey Questionnaire
© 1993 Linda Raney Wright

This survey can be used for either fact-gathering or evangelism. Explain that you are gathering information for a project and seeking honest answers. Ask a potential surveyee if he/she would be willing to relate how they really feel and think about their life and spirituality. The following questions are starter questions.

1. What is important to you? Why?

2. What kinds of things make you happy? Sad?

3. When you hear the word "spiritual" what do you think? Have you had a spiritual journey? What was it?

4. What do you think about spiritual/religious people? Why?

5. What do you think of when you hear the words "life" and "death"? What do you think about life? Your life? What do you think about death? Your own death?

6. What do you want the most from life? Why? Someone has said, "Life is short. Death is sure." How does that make you feel?

7. What do you feel when you think about God? Have you ever tried to communicate with (whatever you think is) God? What happened?

8. On what basis do you make decisions? How do you know if a decision is a good one?

9. Where do you get your values? With so much change and discrepancy in people's values, how do you handle the differences?

10. What do you do when you fail at your own standards? Do you have guilt? How do you deal with it? Have you ever experienced shame or feelings of inadequacy? How do you handle these?

11. What do you think about religion? About specific religions? About Christianity?

12. What kinds of things do you fear? Why?

13. When you hear about satanic rites, witches, demons, spirits, what do you think?

14. What do you think about creation? How did we get here? What do you think about your own creation? Your uniqueness? Where did you come from? Why do you think you are alive?

15. Do you have a sense of dignity, of worth? If so, where does it come from? If not, why not?

16. If there were a knowable God who loved you, supported you, forgave you, listened to you, and helped you, would you want to know him?

17. What do you think about Jesus?

Audience Analysis
© 1993 Linda Raney Wright

Successful communication requires an understanding of what your audience is thinking and why they think that way. You never just speak; you speak to an audience. You never just communicate; you dialogue with a particular person. Good communication starts with an understanding of yourself, your audience, and your message.

The following chart is designed to help you think through how to adapt personal communication or a lecture to your particular personal audience. This chart is not meant to be exhaustive, inflexible, or absolute, but it should stimulate your thoughts concerning how to communicate more effectively.

Characteristics of Audience/Person	Suggested Approach
	A. Intellect
1. Low Intelligence/ Educational Level	a. Understand the underlying emotions: uncertain, possibly low self-esteem, eager to be accepted.
	b. Speaker can draw more conclusions and make more decisions for individual(s).
	c. Can be initially stronger on absolutes.

d. Can be more direct ("you need . . .").

e. Can appeal to peer groups and relationships and be more personal in approach (but maintain academic/truth excellence).

2. High Intelligence/ Educational Level

a. Underlying emotions: proud, self-esteem, take-you-or-leave-you attitude.

b. Present a high level of research and presentation (including quotes, facts, apologetics, logic, historical evidence, etc.).

c. Salt audience with evidence (let them draw their own conclusions). If conclusion is drawn for listener make sure it is obvious to listener *before* an *absolute* statement is given, or else *suggest* conclusion or *ask question*. "When facts are considered, a person might ask, 'Was Jesus God?' "

d. Initially communicate indirectly. Instead of "You need God," try "Many people find that God is the answer to their lives. What do you think? On what do you base this decision?"

e. Avoid strong, absolute statements, generalizations, exaggeration, etc.

f. Be intellectually stimulating. An intelligent person seeks conversation that is not boring, repetitive, or tedious.

3. Free-thinking Attitude (new-age, super tolerant, and passive: any idea is a good one).

a. Understand the underlying emotions: guilt, fear, confusion, dysfunction.

b. Emphasize loving, knowable God, forgiveness.

c. Conversation or speech should be friendly, relationship oriented, emphasizing agreement, very slowly moving to concrete ideas.

4. Intellectually Prejudiced Attitude

a. Underlying emotions usually include anger, pride, and fear.

b. Confident and reasonable communication.

c. Use sources and ideas with which audience/person clearly agrees.

d. Open points of difference with questions, suggestions, and positive statements.

5. Social/Traditional (intellect is incidental to having a good time)

Maintain intellectual credibility but concentrate on personal areas (see low intellectual level).

B. Psychological Status

1. Apathetic (doesn't want to be stimulated, bothered, or responsible)

a. Underlying emotions include: fear, powerlessness, helplessness, loneliness.

b. Show that becoming a Christian is simple.

c. Ask for a minimal commitment (not heavy challenges).

d. Avoid "change the world" emphasis.

e. Emphasize what Christ can do for *them*. Show how Christ can make life happier, more peaceful, secure, and confident.

2. Radical/Idealistic

a. Underlying emotions: empathetic, need to be needed, easily bored.

b. Tell how one can help other people and better our world.

c. Present "Jesus, the Revolutionary."

d. Use the "come help change the world" or "invest your life" appeal.

e. Focus on the kind of person Christ can make: leaders, one with answers, whole.

4. Materialistic

a. Underlying emotions: the need to be somebody, be loved and accepted.

b. Emphasize how they can be loved and accepted.

c. Emphasize status in Christ: child of God, reigning with him, etc.

5. Self-indulgent

a. Underlying emotions: self-hate, helpless, powerless, avoiding pain, no direction.

b. Stress that Christ accepts unconditionally, forgives, restores self-respect, and power to live.

6. Making Mark on Society (grades, position)

a. Underlying emotions: self-confident, pressured by family, need to overcome some element of family history, enjoys being on top.

b. Emphasize how God can help a person reach his potential.

c. Show that God can help with pressure, fear of what others think, opposition, etc.

d. Quote leading Christians in media, sports, political arena, etc.

7. Peer/Group Oriented

a. Underlying emotions: need to be loved, valued, and accepted.

b. Focus on the contemporary and popular rise in Christianity, world wide.

c. Show that Christianity is socially acceptable; quote Christian leaders in media, business, politics, sports, music, etc.

8. Overwhelmed

a. Don't feed lots of information.

b. Present Christianity simply: God's love and help, dumping our burdens on him, a listening ear, a guide.

9. Antagonistic

a. Underlying emotions: anger, disappointments, hopeless, low self-esteem, prideful.

b. Agree life is baffling and complex, many disappointments.

c. Share personal story and the love of God transcending the hurts and pain of life.

C. Needs

1. Self-esteem   Stress a person's value and importance to God.

2. Friendship   Stress love in the Christian community.

3. Need to Be Needed   Explain how they can be a part of the solution.

4. Meaning, Purpose   Emphasize that the person can understand what life is about and how he/she fits in.

5. Hope   Focus on eternal life, present direction, promise of abundant living, etc.

6. Security   Stress that God is with him/her helping, protecting, giving direction, etc.

7. Direction   Show how God gives wisdom for decisions, help in working out personal problems, help in choosing a mate, vocation, friends, etc.

8. Love   a. Make sure your manner and presentation reflect an attitude of love and acceptance.

        b. Present God's love.

Note: If your testimony or the story of a friend is relevant, this would be a great help in illustrating these areas.

D. Morals

1. No Absolutes

a. Underlying emotions: guilt, pain, anger, fear.

b. Be sensitive on the subject of absolutes. Stick to *basics*. Emphasize individual conscience and variety within Christian community on certain issues.

c. Give answers—forgiveness, healing, love, and hope—before insisting on absolute.

d. Show value of living with God's kind of certainty.

2. Absolutes

Initially appeal to absolutes *they* hold to. Reason toward the gospel using their absolutes.

E. Issues

Thinks you're a good or bad person (your message is good or bad) depending on what you state on other issues

Use personal, campus, and national issues for illustrations. Do not raise controversial issues to illustrate gospel. Avoid polarizing issues such as homosexuality, abortion, evolution, politics. Four options if issues become (or are) obstacles to gospel:

1. Choose your fight (i.e., consider avoiding some issues for the sake of the gospel).

2. Don't let right hand know what left hand is doing. (a) Do not bring up controversial issues while witnessing. (b) If you take strong stands on issues do not let it become an obstacle to reaching those to whom God has called you to evangelize and disciple.

3. Explain positions on issues in non-polarizing positive terms.

4. Agree to disagree.

F. Heroes

Make decisions based on others' opinions

a. Underlying emotions: insecurity, uncertainty.

b. Quote people (Christian and non-Christian) whom they respect.

c. Do not directly challenge or belittle their viewpoint.

G. Major Religious Groups

1. Carnal Christians

a. Use a fresh approach to the Christian message. (Many are immune to "Christianese.")

b. Emphasize a personal relationship with God and freedom in Christ (as opposed to legalism).

c. Emphasize the power to live the Christian life (as opposed to self-effort).

d. Use the three circles to describe natural, carnal, and spiritual persons.

e. Stress forgiveness.

2. Catholics

a. Stress a "relationship" with God, not religion.

b. Emphasize a positive view of God (personal, caring, knowable).

c. Emphasize Jesus' human and loving attributes.

d. Stress forgiveness and security (by asking Jesus Christ into your life as Savior once and for all).

e. Point to the world-wide change in the Catholic church where God and Bible have become more personal.

f. Quote Catholic Christians: Pope, Bishop Fulton Sheen, Mother Teresa.

3. Jewish People	a. Recognize strong family bond and cultural ties.
	b. Use Old Testament quotes and illustrations, and messianic prophecies concerning Jesus. Much of New Testament was written by Jews.
	c. Encourage them to ask questions and praise them for any seeking they demonstrate.
	d. Avoid red flag words: "Christ" (use "Jesus"), "convert," "cross," "church," "Old Testament" (use "Hebrew Scriptures"), "Jew" (use "Jewish person").
	e. Emphasize finding Jesus as Messiah is not a change but a completion.
	f. Emphasize caring Christian "family" of believers.
4. Members of Eastern Religions/ New Age	a. Underlying emotions: Many turn to this illogical approach to life because they have given up trying to make sense of their world, or they are curious, looking for something new, or do not have answers for "guilt" feelings, or are seeking personal power, etc.

b. Show Christianity as progressive, stimulating, and powerful.

c. Include testimonies of converted mystics.

d. Emphasize the historicity, transcendence, personal nature, and love of Christianity.

e. Show that Jesus was uniquely deity (trilemma, resurrection) and can give power ("I can do all things through Christ"), mental growth, deep truths, personal victory, freedom from guilt.

5. Members of Cults

a. Underlying emotions: many choose cults because of the simplicity of having someone else define their lives; or, they are looking for a group to be a part of, acceptance, security, or a systematic thought process to alleviate uncertainty or fear.

b. Emphasize the family group of Christians.

c. Emphasize that God helps one know life and how to make decisions; that a perfect person, God, can reside within you and is superior to a group. The Holy Spirit becomes our stability.

d. Emphasize the solid structure of Christianity.

e. Emphasize security, friendship and forgiveness.

f. Don't argue minor points; keep the focus on Jesus, security, love, and certainty.

H. Perception

If your listener perceives you/Christians in a negative way what focus and communication can be offered to remove this "caricature" barrier? Possible perceptions of Christians by non-Christians include:

1. Parental/Superior Attitude

a. Focus: one beggar telling another beggar where to find bread. "In which you formerly walked, according to the course of this world."

b. Communication: "I would like to share what made a difference to me. I respect your right to make your own decisions."

2. Pushy/Controlling

a. Focus: It is the Spirit's job to convict of sin, righteousness, and judgment.

b. Communication: "I'm not trying to force my views on you but merely wish to give you some information for your consideration."

3. Angry

a. Focus: "Grievous words stir up anger." "Let your communication be seasoned with grace."

b. Communication: Center on Jesus as loving and accepting.

4. Judgmental

a. Focus: "All have sinned and fallen short of God's glory." "Love covers a multitude of sins."

b. Communication: "I am aware that life's decisions are difficult and that you are most likely giving it your all to do your best. May I suggest a few things that have helped me. You no doubt have many ideas that could benefit me as well."

Resource List

Books:

500 Jokes and Humorous Stories . . . and How to Tell Them! (Formerly *Secrets of Successful Humor.*) Zig Ziglar says, "What a delight, what a pleasure to read! [This book tells us] how we can adapt humor . . . to fit our specific situation." Use it for public speaking, with small groups, one-to-one. How to tell humorous stories with a punch; what to do when it bombs. "You'll laugh as you learn," says Dick Van Dyke. 224 pages, paper. $5.95

Good Days, Bad Days/Hope for the Sick and Hurting. Coping with sickness requires physical, psychological, and spiritual resources. Does God always heal? Does he ever heal? What if I can't get well? Balanced, biblical encouragement and guidance for those who hurt . . . and those who care for them. Crossover book written to Christians and non-Christians. 253 pages. $10.95

Spiritual Warfare and Evangelism. A balanced, biblical guide for dealing with the forces of darkness that attack evangelistic efforts. Learn to use the authority that is yours as a child of God! 44 pages, paper. Bulk discounts available. $5.00

Staying on Top When Things Go Wrong, by Linda Raney Wright. How to see yourself the way God see you. Positive self-image, dealing with discouragement, pursuing your dreams and trusting God through it all. ". . . concepts that, if applied, provide a full and meaningful life." —Vonette Zachary Bright. 125 pages, mass paper. $3.95

Success Helper. Condensed version of *Staying on Top.* 71 pages, mass paper. Bulk discounts available. $2.50

Raising Children, by Linda Raney Wright. Ruth Graham, Vonette Bright, Arvella Schuller, Evelyn Christenson, and eight other mothers invite you into their homes to share their successes, their failures, and answers they've found in raising children. Revised edition, 190 pages, mass paper. $3.95

Raising Children (first edition). Excellent gift! 158 pages, quality paper. $3.00

A Cord of Three Strands. Biblical treatise on women in the home and community. $10.99

University Classroom Lecturing. Need to prepare a Christian talk on a contemporary topic? Here's a great starting place! Documented outlines for over fifty talks ranging from apologetics to abortion, self-image to sex. Includes bibliography, questions to anticipate, plus additional helps. Appropriate for classrooms (university and high school), evangelistic talks, free speech, Sunday school instruction, church sermons, discussion groups, etc. Over 400 pages.

Communications Principles Training Manual. Training manual for popular course on evangelistic public speaking. How to analyze your audience and prepare and present speeches that clearly relate Christ to topics of secular interest. 65 pages.

Videos:

Jesus and Gender: What Jesus Did for Women, with Linda Raney Wright. A refreshing look at Jesus' attitudes, assertions, and accomplishments concerning women. Skillfully presented with the non-Christian in mind and also contains a tactful gospel presentation. $18.00

Communications Principles Training I. Spiritual warfare and Evangelism. How to recognize the schemes of the Enemy of our souls and how to confront him in God's power. Introduction to CPT, the Wrights' popular course in evangelistic public speaking. How to approach professors and line up classroom lectures. $18.00

Communications Principles Training II. Audience Analysis. What interests your audience most? Turn it into a gateway for the gospel. How to prepare and present lectures for maximum impact. A focus on university lecturing principles that relate to nearly any public speaking. *Note: These two videos are most effective when used with the companion "Communications Principles Training Manual."* $18.00

Tapes (audio):

Communication Principles Training, by Linda Raney Wright. Training from the Wrights' successful communications course. How to analyze your audience and prepare and present speeches that win. Three-tape set. $10.00

Spiritual Warfare and Evangelism, by Linda Raney Wright. Practical how to's in exercising your authority as a believer over the spiritual Enemy in evangelism. Picks up where the book leaves off. You can win! $4.00

Women in Evangelism, by Linda Raney Wright. If we want to reach the whole world for Christ, we must use the whole work force. Understanding women's roles in the Great Commission. $4.00

Please Send Me:

Quantity	Title	Price
Books		
___	500 Jokes and Humorous Stories . . . and How to Tell Them!	5.95
___	Good Days, Bad Days/ Hope for the Sick and Hurting	10.95
___	Spiritual Warfare and Evangelism	5.00
___	Staying on Top When Things Go Wrong	3.95
___	Success Helper	2.50
___	Raising Children (revised edition)	3.95
___	Raising Children (first edition)	3.00
___	A Cord of Three Strands	10.99
___	University Classroom Lecturing	25.50
___	Communication Principles Manual	8.00
Videos		
___	Jesus and Gender: What Jesus Did for Women (evangelistic)	18.00
___	Communications Principles Training I	18.00
___	Communications Principles Training II	18.00

Tapes (audio)

___	Communication Principles Training	10.00
___	Spiritual Warfare and Evangelism	4.00
___	Women in Evangelism	4.00

Subtotal $_____

Indianaa residents: multiply by 0.05 tax $_____

Shipping and Handling: Subtotal x 0.15 $_____
(International orders add 25% for surface
or 50% for air shipping. Call, fax, or write
for bulk order shipping charges.)

Total $_____

___ Enclosed is my check for $_____ made payable to
Integrated Resources.

___ Please send videos in (check one):
__NTSC __PAL

Ship to: Name _____

Address_____
_____
_____
_____
_____

Please complete form and send with check or account
transfer to:

Integrated Resources   Or Call 1-800-729-4351 ext. 7700
4307 East Third St.   (812) 339-8388 ext. 7700
Bloomington, IN 47401   Fax (812) 339-8389
U.S.A.

If unavailable contact:

> Linda Wright
> P.O. Box 1566
> Crestline, CA 92325

For information or phone/credit card orders call:

> 1-800-729-4351
> 1-812-339-8388

Correspondence to author may be directed to:

Linda Wright Ministry
P.O. Box 1566
Crestline, CA 92325
U.S.A.
1-909-338-4483